Modern Photojournalism

Tim N. Gidal

Modern Photojournalism

Origin and Evolution, 1910-1933

Collier Books

A Division of Macmillan Publishing Co., Inc.

New York

Modern Photojournalism: Origin and Evolution, 1910-1933 is
Volume 1 of
PHOTOGRAPHY: MEN AND MOVEMENTS
Edited by Romeo E. Martinez

Macmillan Publishing Co., Inc.
866 Third Avenue, New York N.Y. 10022
Collier-Macmillan Canada Ltd., Toronto, Ontario

Library of Congress Catalog Card Number: 73-10788

Modern Photojournalism: Origin and Evolution, 1910-1933
is also published in a hardcover
edition by Macmillan Publishing Co., Inc.

First Collier Books Edition 1973

English translation by Maureen Oberli-Turner
Printed in Switzerland

Foreword

Photojournalism, as the word implies, is a visual expansion of journalism. But whereas the concept of journalism is related to the area of the daily newspaper, photojournalism is, generally speaking, the main support of the illustrated weekly magazines. Modern photojournalism, however, is chiefly manifested in photoreportages, photostories, and photoessays.

Modern photoreportage originated in Germany between 1928 and 1931. Three main factors caused its breakthrough: the development of the modern 35 mm camera (above all the Leica) and of the Ermanox; the emergence of a new generation of photoreporters who opened up new areas of photoreportage with the aid of highly sensitive new equipment; and the attitude assumed by the editors of the illustrated magazines who were prepared to experiment and became the creative originators of this new medium of mass communication. Still more important is the fact that photoreportage took its cues not from art or literature, but from the many and varied aspects of the *condition humaine* itself. The emphasis was placed almost exclusively on the human element. The new photojournalism became a medium of human communication directed primarily toward the individual in the mass rather than the mass instinct in the individual. In addition, unlike the area of art, photoreportage is not the expression of a projected inner vision, but a documentary report on reality. The "personal touch" is not an integral part of genuine photoreportage; the statement is formed by experienced facts. It should be remembered that sensationalism and indiscretion have no place in true photojournalism.

"Sensational," wrote Heinrich Böll, "this picture of the little Chinese boy bending seriously over his bowl of rice!" This criterion applied to the photoreporter complies—although from an entirely different standpoint—with Plato's criticism of the artist, in which he accused him of creating nothing but reproductions of the outer world. In these two statements, the roles of the artist and the photoreporter are clearly defined: whereas the artist's role is to express his inner vision in a visual form, the photoreporter's task is to present an image of the factual, tangible world.

It is the photoreporter who determines the essential content of the photoreportage, but he is also dependent on an accompanying text and a corresponding layout of his pictures. Thus the editor of the illustrated magazine is a genuine creative artist who, far from merely adding, establishes an order out of his basic concept, resulting in a harmonious entity which, in its turn, adds to the sum of the individual parts.

A fact which is not an accident. In addition to the objectivity imposed by studying the source material, subjective elements are also evident in this report on the beginnings of photojournalism. By this means, the author hopes to provide the reader with a closeness to happenings and events that he himself experienced firsthand.

I should like to take this opportunity to express heartfelt thanks to my friend and mentor Stefan Lorant—the motor force of modern photojournalism—for his invaluable information and advice.

I. Forerunners and Beginnings

From an historical point of view, modern photoreportage is the contemporary form of the pictorial report, which employs the technical means of its time to accomplish the age-old task of visual communication. The content, limits, and purposes of the report are determined by the direct or indirect statement itself, and it is this which also imposes a limit on propagandistic exaggeration and falsification, as well as on the purely imaginative element which exists in the film report and the comic strip. Thus defined, the documentary content of the photographic report is a visual historical documentation of the events, social conditions, culture, and civilization—as well as the barbarism and lack of culture—of a given time. Didactically defined, it is the instigator of political agitation.

"Yo lo vi" scribbled Goya under one of his gruesome war scenes of the battles between the Spanish partisans and the Napoleonic troops in 1810: "This I saw!" The etching depicts a vain attempt at flight from a burning village. Other pictures show massacres and rapes by French soldiers. Goya reports the objective facts with graphic and subjective passion—events he witnessed and which he portrays with anything but distance and indifference. His pictures are like the cry of the martyr. The unmistakable characteristics of the painter, together with the technical elements of the copper plate and the etching process, serve as filters between three-dimensional events and their two-dimensional representation.

While the painter *interprets* events and happenings, the photographer is able to *reflect* them in a precise and accurate form. The choice of the *content* of the report remains subjective, however, and the human element of selection cannot be eliminated. It is still the human being who reports, but the invention of photography and the photographic report excludes the technical means of the painter. The *Yo lo vi* is made credible by the mechanical process of the camera lens and the film. But even now, photoreportage gains in substance and veracity when the photoreporter who observes the world through his camera lens and captures what he sees and experiences is genuinely committed to his task. The documentary confirmation of the photoreporter's "That's how it was" is identical to Goya's "This I saw." Eliminated now is the necessity of the subjective mediums of woodcuts, copper plates, or lithographs—the graphic conversion of event into representation. Thus the documentary report has not only become a practical possibility, it has also been liberated from the limits of graphic conversion.

Naturally enough, the photoreporter also reports on new and interesting facts and events, both entertaining and educational, as did the illustrated magazines of the nineteenth century. But, if the photoreporter is to be worthy of

1855 Crimean War: Balaklava.
Photo: Roger Fenton

his camera, he must identify himself with the human problems which, tangibly or intangibly, have to form the basic core of his work. The genuine reporter—and by this we mean the rare phenomenon of the passionately committed photojournalist—personally experiences what he captures on film: laughter and tears, joy and sorrow, tragedy and comedy. It is only through his subjective experience of the objective facts that the photoreporter can become a witness to his time. His alertness and his gift of observation distinguish his work from that of others—not as an artist, but related to the artist by virtue of this talent of creative observation.

Modern photojournalism began in full force in Germany in 1928 and 1929, although its visible harbingers can be established a few years earlier. It reached fruition in 1933 and 1934, above all in Germany. Subsequently it expanded and joined up with its most important representatives in Paris, Amsterdam, London, and New York—in flight from the psychological repression and physical persecution in Nazi Germany.

Isolated forerunners of photoreportage existed much earlier, however. Barely fifteen years after the invention of practical photography by Niepce, Daguerre, and Talbot, the Englishman Roger Fenton created a magnificent photographic report on the siege and conquest of Sebastopol during the Crimean War in 1855. Fenton had to overcome enormous difficulties since his light-sensitive material consisted of 700 glass plates, most of them measuring 12×16 inches. Each plate had to be covered with the necessary chemicals in the transportable darkroom before exposure, and Fenton succeeded in bringing approximately 350 photographs back to England. The wet plates ("wet process") had to be developed immediately following exposure, and the length of the exposure varied from three to twenty seconds. Close-ups of human subjects had to be posed, owing to the limited sensitivity of the plates and the lenses. Fenton knew how to select suitable scenes and to arrest the action only for the length of the exposure. It was not the camera which "froze" the action, as is the case today, but it was the photographer himself who arrested the movement for three to twenty seconds.

Even though the greater part of Fenton's pictures were posed, the officers and soldiers nevertheless behaved with great naturalness in the presence of his giant camera. Fenton's talent of not destroying the natural atmosphere of the moment by unnatural poses and grouping lent his pictures an element of naturalness which is still valid today. He possessed the qualities of the "born" photoreporter, and we only have to compare his pictures with those of his colleagues from the same period to realize that the element of the ridiculous—appealing though it may sometimes be—is entirely absent from his work by virtue of its absolute naturalness. It is already evident from his pictures that the genuine photoreporter is not bound to fashionable manners of presentation or style, nor to an inimitable individual style. Fenton's undeniable aim, conscious or unconscious, was the reproduction of that which he and his camera had seen and experienced.

Fenton's photographs appeared in huge folio volumes, into which the original prints were pasted, and were published by the London publisher Thomas Agnew. As mechanical reproduction of the photos in newspapers had not yet become possible, many of Fenton's pictures served as originals for woodcuts which first appeared in *The London Illustrated News*. Subsequently they were printed in European magazines—the *Leipziger Illustrirte* and *L'Illustration* (Paris)—and the American journals *Frank Leslie's Illustrated Newspaper* (Boston) and *Harper's Weekly* (New York). But even without these indirect reproductions in the weeklies, Roger Fenton's photographs of the Crimean War were a genuine photoreportage.

This comprehensive photoreportage deals with life in war, a subject which, from the photographer's point of view, is as worthwhile as it is dangerous. But Fenton's pictures of the Crimean War did not represent the first photoreportage. This distinction falls to a report of an expedition which comprises around eight hundred daguerreotypes. In 1852, the United States government commissioned two daguerreotypers to photograph American naval vessels at anchor off Yokohama in February 1854 under Commodore Matthew Calbraith Perry. Shortly afterward, a treaty which opened up two harbors for American shipping was drawn up between Commodore Perry and the Japanese government. Thus Japan was forced to open its doors to American trade and subsequently to Western trade in general, and—although a side effect—the Western world thus was opened to Japanese trade.

The daguerreotypes were copied in woodcuts and lithographs and were published in illustrated magazines. One

1860 Confusion in China; the Captured Fort of Pehtang.
Photo: Felice A. Beato

of the originals by the photographer E. Brown is still in existence in Japan. The others are probably in the possession of a state archive in Washington—awaiting a sensational rediscovery. Each photograph, unlike Fenton's glass plates, was a positive from which it was not possible to make further prints.

Comprehensive photoreportages appeared next between 1861 and 1865. Mathew Brady, his collaborators Alexander Gardner, Timothy H. O'Sullivan, and their assistants documented the American Civil War in thousands of photographs from its beginning to the funeral of Abraham Lincoln. Fenton's reportage was a report on life in war. This American reportage was a horrifying document of death in war—an account of death in all its naked realism.

Brady's photographs also reveal the technical deficiencies of early photography: long exposures, heavy cameras, and the wet process completely robbed the pictures of spontaneity. In spite of this, Brady's assertions in his catalogue that the photos were taken during the Civil War and that they depicted its true grimness were thoroughly justified.

1863 The war between the States: Gettysburg battlefield.
Photo: T. H. O'Sullivan (1840–1882)

1865 Execution of conspirators against President Lincoln.
Photo: Alexander Gardner (1821–1882)
Collection: Tim Gidal

The seventies saw the emergence of the dry plate, and in 1878, the first serviceable snapshot was taken with an exposure of 1/25th of a second. At the same time, the smaller and handier camera was rapidly developing; the small "detective camera" became fashionable, and in 1888 George Eastman in Rochester brought the first Kodak box camera onto the market. This camera measured approximately 3 1/4 × 3 × 6 1/2 inches and used a roll of film which took 100 circular pictures of approximately 2 1/4 inches in diameter each.

In France, too, a number of cameras were in the process of development, and it was there that Paul Nadar made the first photointerview with his *vélocigraphe*. He took the pictures, and his father—the brilliant and intrepid photographer, Nadar senior (Gaspard-Félix Tournachon)—interviewed, with the help of a shorthand writer, the professor of chemistry, Eugène Chevreuil, on the theme of "The Art of Living Longer." (Chevreuil lived to the ripe old age of 103, from 1786 to 1889.) The interview appeared in *Le Petit Journal illustré*. Paul Nadar specialized in interviewing well-known personalities in their surroundings, and his work in this field includes reportage-like photointerviews with General Boulanger, Gustave Eiffel, and Louis Pasteur. This was the beginning of the photointerview.

1876–1878 Famine in Madras, India.
Photo: W. W. Hooper

The time of the long exposure, even outdoors, was now over. In 1840, the Viennese mathematician Joseph Petzval made a 1 : 3.4 lens, giving a light intensity six times stronger than Daguerre's landscape lens. In 1861, William England invented the focal-plane shutter, which made it possible to take pictures with exposures of 1/20th to 1/1200th of a second (or at least it would have been possible if the sensitive plates necessary for this had been available). The sensitivity of the plates increased only slowly, however.

The most important development of the time was the photomechanical reproduction of pictures on newsprint by halftone. In 1880, the New York newspaper *Daily Graphic* published the first photograph reproduced from the original by a mechanical process based on breaking up the photograph into minute particles by means of a screen of crossed lines placed in front of the photographic negative. The image was then transferred through the screened negative onto a metal block, and it was from this block that the photograph was printed together with the typographic text. Here was the first publication of a photograph in the printing process via halftone photoengraving. "We have dealt heretofore with pictures made with drawings or engravings. Here we have one direct from nature.... We are still experimenting with it, and feel confident that our experiments will in the long run result in success, and that pictures will eventually be regularly printed in our pages direct from photographs without the intervention of drawing" (quoted from Beaumont Newhall).

This first halftone picture to appear in a newspaper was the work of Stephen Henry Horgan. Two years later, the process was improved by Georg Meisenbach in Munich, Germany. His contribution was the breakdown of the image into minute squares. The dry plate, the focal-plane shutter, and the halftone block represented the birth of the documentary photograph which could be printed directly. Nevertheless, almost fifty years were to pass before technical progress and the demands of the time created modern photoreportage within the meaning of modern photojournalism. Another important factor was that with the exception of Brady and his assistants, none of the forerunners of photoreportage was a professional photographer. They were lawyers, doctors, engineers, scientists—as were, indeed, the first modern photoreporters later on.

The themes of war, expeditions, and interviews were soon joined by socio-analytic photographic reports. The technical possibility of shorter exposures was at last at hand, and photographs taken out-of-doors without the aid of a tripod were now perfectly possible. Flash powder, invented in 1887, eliminated the difficulty of indoor exposures and outdoor exposures in poor lighting conditions. The process consisted of igniting magnesium powder on an open metal surface while the camera shutter was open. The method resulted in a good many fires and explosions. The newspaper king, William Randolph Hearst, forbade the use of flash powder after a reporter lost an arm in an accident caused by an explosion—just one year before the flash bulb came onto the market in 1930.

The simplified technical process made it possible to concentrate the camera lens on close-ups and human subjects, although little advantage was taken of this fact at first. The masterly handling of the camera which resulted from technical developments was still decades away—the long road taken by a slave of camera technique to the mastery of his equipment. All the more impressive are the achievements of the American photographers Jacob August Riis and Lewis W. Hine—probably the first to express the spirit of social protest through the medium of photoreportage.

Jacob August Riis emigrated to America from his native Denmark. After the first few difficult years in the new country, he was employed in 1877 as a police reporter on the famous *New York Tribune*. Riis' "hunting ground" was provided by the East Side slums where he often wandered between two and four o'clock in the morning in order to observe the inhabitants "off guard" in their foul-smelling streets and even fouler dwellings. He first published his report in the *Tribune*, and subsequently in the *Evening Sun*. The echo was only weak—incredible when we consider that Riis described scenes such as that of twelve men and women sleeping in a room of approximately 54 square feet, most of them on the floor, and hundreds of men, women, and children slowly starving to death in their foul dwellings. It was his aim to abolish these "pigsties" as soon as it was humanly possible.

Riis quickly learned to handle his camera and flash with great skill, and the fact that half the population was unwilling to believe his descriptions of how the other half lived impelled him to document his words by means of photographs.

The flash powder of the "frying pan" had to be ignited like a revolver shot, and this inevitably awoke the populace. This resulted in considerable unpleasantness, and Riis set two houses on fire and almost lost his sight. But he refused to give up, and in 1890 the first of his protest books, *How the Other Half Lives*, was published. It described the living conditions of over one million inhabitants of New York, most of whom lacked the absolute minimum means to live and had no possibility or hope of ever obtaining it. Thousands of them were forced to earn a meager living as thieves, prostitutes, pimps, and criminals.

VOR 50 JAHREN:

Ein Grosspapa des Giftgaskrieges wird fotografiert

Der alte Herr rechts und auf den anderen Bildern ist sozusagen ein Großpapa des Giftgaskrieges, der berühmte franz. Chemiker Chevreuil, den der findige Fotograf Nadar im Jahre 1886 besuchte. Nadar hat den Verlauf dieses Besuches in einer Reihe von Fotografien festgehalten, die an Schärfe, Lebendigkeit und Situationstreue den fotografischen Aufnahmen unserer Zeit nicht nachstehen. Diese Fotos stellen zugleich eine der ersten neuzeitlichen Bildberichterstattungen dar, die Form der starren Aufnahme ist durch die Verbesserung der Apparatetechnik durchbrochen. Der Fotograf braucht die Aufmerksamkeit nicht mehr auf seine Vorbereitungen zu lenken, er fotografiert jetzt in dem Augenblick, indem er sein Aufnahmeobjekt in seinem natürlichsten Ausdruck findet. Das Ergebnis seiner

1886 *Interview with the French scientist M. E. Chevreuil.*
Photos: Felix and Paul Nadar

1888 *Bandit's Roost, Mulberry Street, New York.*
Photo: Jacob A. Riis (1849–1914)

1905 Italian immigrants on Ellis Island.
Photo: Lewis W. Hine (1874–1940)

As halftone photoengraving was still in its infancy, only seventeen photos were printed by this process in *How the Other Half Lives*, and nineteen photographs were reproduced as line drawings. But even these few documents caused enough indignation to provide the basis of social reform.

Riis' most important successor was the sociologist Lewis W. Hine. To him the camera (5 × 7-inch format) represented a form of concrete evidence for his university studies, and with it he pursued the new immigrants from the Ellis Island quarantine station to their wretched dwellings. He took pictures of children working twelve hours at a stretch in the cotton factories of the South for a starvation wage; he showed the wretched working and living conditions of the miners. Hine's *Photo-Stories* appeared in good halftone print—with the result that a revision was made in the laws relating to child labor. He was a reformer whose tool was the camera, and he was well aware that the subjective element in his pictures, far from detracting from their documentary value, considerably strengthened it. He possessed a personal commitment which made it possible for him to make a great and lasting contribution to the direction of public criticism of the economic system as it related to the huge mass of underprivileged persons. Hine's intentions were twofold: he wanted to show things which must be abolished, and he wanted to show what should be recognized and appreciated.

Meanwhile, the popularity of the camera had increased steadily. It was used by thousands of professional photographers and tens of thousands of amateurs. It was also an essential part of the equipment of an expedition. The North Pole explorer, Robert Edwin Peary, for example, brought some dramatic documentary photos back from his voyage of discovery in 1909, a number of which were published. They showed the endless march in the often sunless ice desert, the perilous and wearisome crossings over ice hills and fissures, and the joyful triumph at the journey's end. Amusing photos of the life of the Eskimos were also included, with Eskimo girls dancing on the deck of the ship, as well as a series of nude pictures.

If it is true to say that Riis and Hine tended to depict the disadvantaged side of life, it was left to the French gentleman and amateur reporter Jacques-Henri Lartigue to produce a document in reportage style of the life of French high society in his *Photo-Diary of Our Century*, a volume of great charm and high sensitivity.

Heinrich Zille, an artist concerned mainly with making drawings of the Berlin milieu, took some impressive photographs of this subject between 1908 and 1911.

Riis, Hine, Lartigue, and Zille were genuine forerunners of modern photoreportage. Together with two or three others, they stand out among the innumerable press photographers who achieved professional status in the late nineties. The illustrated magazines quickly recognized the new possibilities provided by the mechanical reproduction of photos together with written copy. The photographs served as an illustrative complement to the text, an additional source of information, a technical alleviation and shortening of the work process, and a higher source of income. At first, however, the introduction of the printed photograph was thought to have lowered the standard of

1909 Robert Edwin Peary's North Pole expedition.

The erection of the Bavaria in Munich (1850).
Photo: Alois Löcherer

the magazines, since the previous hand-illustrated reportages which were executed in a fine naturalistic technique had greatly contributed to the popularity of weeklies such as the *Illustrated London News*, Weber's *Leipziger Illustrirte Zeitung*, the French *L'Illustration*, *Harper's Weekly*, and *Frank Leslie's Illustrated Newspaper* in America. For the way in which the draftsman and the wood-engraver were able to depict the observed facts and events remained technically impossible for the photographer for many decades. Thus picture reportage disappeared from the scene, except in cases where it survived in the form of reproductions of drawings. Nevertheless, the established magazines were joined by a number of new journals, and 1890 saw the foundation of the *Berliner Illustrirte Zeitung,* a magazine with a circulation of 14,000 copies in the first year, one million in 1914, and two million in 1930. In 1899 *Die Woche* appeared on the scene, and this too reached a high circulation. Both magazines were illustrated, almost throughout, with single photographs combined with the text, and sometimes whole themes were represented by photographs. Now and then, a series of photographs provided by traveling reporters from distant countries was published. Here, too, the emphasis lay on the photograph as an illustration of the text. The editorial section consisted mainly of text.

Socially speaking, the photographer was placed somewhere between the employee and skilled worker. Equipped with folding camera, flash, and tripod, he took pictures of society wedding guests, participants at conferences, inspections of troops, royal and imperial visits, fleets and military parades, as well as studio portraits of potentates, scientists, artists, politicians, writers, actors, and singers. These pictures indicate a particularly strong element of a "watch-the-birdie" style, which reveals less of the individual subject than of the way he saw, or imagined, himself. According to his profession, the subject would confront the camera with a majestic, soulful, dignified, friendly, thoughtful, serious, or enraptured expression. Actors tended toward the dramatic, comedians to humorous grimaces, and female singers toward a teasing, seductive pose. A number of singers were fond of showing their teeth and open mouths, as if they were on the point of singing a high E. (In the case of animals, the "pose" varied. Horses, cows, deer, giraffes, and llamas stared curiously into the lens; others seemed unconcerned, depending on their relationship to the photographer. On the whole, however, animal photos, both past and present, tend to reveal a certain shyness.)

Apart from popular animal subjects, the photographic illustrated magazines were fond of reporting on sports and sporting events. Here there was a certain spontaneity of pose and expression. For example, it is hardly to be expected that a boxer turn a smiling face to the camera during a fight, or a sprinter or football player "turn on" a relaxed expression in the middle of a competition or match. The technical demands of sports photography had a considerable influence on photography as a whole. The outstanding sports photos by Lothar Rübelt, Munkacsi, and others—taken shortly after World War I and in the early postwar period—clearly revealed the possibility of reproducing the natural facial expression of the subject in photographs in which the subject was unaware of being photographed. The transition from the picture reports, before the invention of the halftone block, to the modern photoreportage was largely brought about by sports reportage and reportages which—though taken from drawings and not from original photographs—no longer involved the troublesome intermediate process of the engraved wooden block but were faithfully reproduced by the photomechanical process, usually with the use of a screen block. However, these reportages were not primarily documentary, as can be seen from the numerous, often propagandistically drawn picture reports of World War I. Here the war was represented as "the father of all things" or as technical progress. A true-to-life report was by no means in accordance with the intentions of the militaristic leaders of the war, and the reports showed inspections of troops, light-hearted soldiers marching past enthusiastic crowds, and the departure of military vehicles bearing humorous inscriptions in German, French, and English announcing their imminent, victorious return.

Admittance to the battlefields was strictly forbidden to press photographers. Only certain selected military photographers were allowed in these areas. This rule was absolutely rigid in the German and French armies; the General Staffs' censorship was inflexible in the extreme. Any attempt to show the true face of the war would have been regarded as a stab in the back of official wartime morale. Thus there were only a very few amateur photos which showed the war in unposed and true-to-life realism. It was only at the end of the war and in the postwar period that picture reportage began its march to victory in the hands of the photoreporter.

II. 1918–1928: The Beginning of an Era and the Quest for a Type of Visual Documentation Appropriate to the Period

Among all the thousands of official and unofficial photographs of World War I, there is one which is well remembered: a column of English soldiers with their eyes bound, each with his hand on the shoulder of the man in front of him, stumbling in single file over a devastated battlefield. Some of them had been blinded by poison gas—an apocalyptic vision of horrors to come in the next war. Any attempt to interpret this picture fails. It is a visual document of man-made reality which tells a lot about World War I—and about wars. No written word could ever hope to reveal the truth more vividly.

After the war came revolutions, first the Russian, then the German. These revolutions were captured in numerous photographs—of street fights, starving people, mass demonstrations, the cruelties of civil war, and the first attempts to begin anew.

Willi Ruge, probably the first reporter-photographer in Germany, captured the street battles in Berlin in many photographs.

The Soviet Russians were the first to develop consciously the propaganda possibilities of the documentary photograph with an eye to agitating the people. Thus documentary photography became a didactic mass medium. The equally didactic captions, together with the pictures, resulted in historic documents or pseudodocuments in which the objective factual evidence was interpreted for propaganda purposes. Propaganda "information," by the definition of Marx and Lenin, was an essential part of the picture report and the tactical consequence of this attitude was the training of over one hundred thousand "worker photographers" in the Soviet Union during postwar years. They were taught to produce "realistic-naturalistic" pictures, optimistic in mood, and to omit any hint of possible deficiencies even when the subject matter dealt with professions. The same was true of comprehensive photoreportages which appeared in the illustrated Soviet papers and in the propagandistic monthly magazine, *USSR in Pictures*, which was distributed in a number of foreign countries, including Germany. "A Day in the Life of the Filipov" was a typical reportage of this kind, and it is quite possible that Solzhenitsyn's ruthless and revealing book, *A Day in the Life of Ivan Denisovich*, was in fact an embittered satire on the rose-colored representation of daily life with which he must have been confronted often enough in magazines during his youth.

In this postwar period, Germany was the scene of all kinds of unrest—inflation, political trials, and assassinations, and also of renewed efforts and hope for a better future. The battle for the unstable Weimar Republic, expressionism in art, literature, theater, and film, the youth movements and the Charleston, and a deep and passionate longing for peace and international fraternization were likewise symptomatic of the twenties. The postwar generation was confronted with a wide variety of new attitudes toward social and aesthetic values. The theaters showed plays by Ibsen, Hauptmann, Gorki, Strindberg, Kaiser, Shakespeare, Shaw, Sternheim, Toller, and Bertolt Brecht. Russian films by Eisenstein and Pudovkin opened up a new world of observation through the medium of the cinema, although the prototypes of the Soviet Russian photoreportages were not so much Eisenstein's heroic films but rather the more domestic, everyday themes of Pudovkin's early productions, such as "The Mother" (1926), and Dziga Vertov's "The Man with the Camera," which portrayed the life of an average Moscow citizen. Vertov was originally a "newsreel man" by profession and regarded the film director as a "pictorial reporter" and the camera lens as his eye. He thus achieved a naturalistic way of seeing, a way of seeing which was particularly evident in Germany in *People on Sunday*, inspired by Moriz Seeler. This film was directed by Robert Siodmak, the book was by Billy Wilder (subsequently a Hollywood director), and the cameraman was Eugen Schüftan. It was filmed without professional actors and was "natural," by way of contrast to exaggeratedly expressionistic films such as *Mabuse, the Gambler* or *The Cabinet of Dr. Caligari*.

"Down with tradition! Photograph things and people as they really are!" was the mood of this new movement. Ideas from East and West came into contact with each other—ideas which were to influence the approaching new photoreportage and thus the new photojournalism. Much has been written about the twenties, much sense and much nonsense—just as the twenties themselves were characterized by sense and nonsense. Were they the "golden twenties," harbinger of the dawn of a new humanity? Today, in retrospect, we know better. Were they the decadent years in which the foul-smelling gases of the coming political and human eruptions of the Nazi empire and

World War II were already developing beneath the surface composed of many glittering and partially mildewed facets?

In retrospect, one thing is certain: World War I represented the end of the bourgeois nineteenth century and the downfall of its social and intellectual values. This world had reached its culmination in the years preceding World War I. It was an optimistic world of economic, technological, and scientific progress in "the best of all possible worlds." Its greatest artistic achievement was cubist painting between 1907 and 1914. With the outbreak of World War I, the politicians and governments destroyed this "best of all possible worlds." A new era began in the postwar world of the twenties—the period between 1924 and 1933—an era in which the world of yesterday had already attained an historical significance and had, at the same time, foundered.

The new world was born out of hope and ridicule, knowledge and error, work and unemployment, disappointment and belief. In the laboratories of a liberated Golem, science and technology made equal contributions in healing and salvation on the one hand and destruction and killing on the other. New mass movements and ideals were born, the harbingers of which were both the printed word and the new mediums of mass communication.

III. The Camera—A Witness of the Times

During these years, a number of mass-media, illustrated magazines came onto the German market—a phenomenon typical only of Germany. The period was visually documented by the photojournalism in these magazines; at the same time, various improvements combined to make the camera an extension of the observant eye. Two cameras came onto the market which had a determining influence on the new photojournalism—the Leica and the Ermanox. Intellectual, economic, and technical factors all played their part in the birth of modern photojournalism.

Press photography by professionals had reached a dead end. On the one hand, it was controlled and restricted by the narrow attitude toward press photography, and on the other hand, by the outmoded equipment and the huge, unwieldy, and intricate plate cameras. Press photographers "knew of nothing better," and the editors of the illustrated magazines also knew nothing—or too little—of the new technical possibilities which had been developing. Apart from this, there was a lack of ideas. There were, of course, exceptions and experiments, above all by the *Berliner Illustrirte* whose editor Kurt Korff and publishing director Kurt Szafranski recognized the dead end which conservative press photography had reached, despite its clearly worthwhile achievements.

One of the exceptions among photographers on the *Berliner Illustrirte* was the Hungarian, Martin Munkacsi. As early as 1923 he brought reportage photographs of a singular beauty back with him from Spain and published them in a comprehensive photoreportage. Like Cartier-Bresson today, Munkacsi was chiefly concerned in a reportage with the quest for individual culminating points and with formal construction. He was a passionate "one-shot reporter" who often succeeded in obtaining outstandingly impressive photos. What Cartier-Bresson says of himself applies also to Munkacsi: he aspired to control the physical nature of the picture by his formal intention and he attempted to capture the essential character of a scene in a perfect picture. These two great photoreporters have something in common, but Cartier-Bresson emphasizes the statement, while Munkacsi was concerned above all with the photographic impact.

An even stronger tendency toward comprehensive and balanced reportage is early evident in the work of Munkacsi's countryman, André Kertesz, who lived at the time in Paris and often worked for German magazines. Kertesz, too, started by taking single photos, but he soon discovered the picture series—an area in which he was a real master, although it represents only a small part of his work. The same applies to the Hungarian, Brassaï, who also lived in Paris.

The year 1921 saw the foundation of the Communist *Arbeiter Illustrierte Zeitung (AIZ)* in Berlin, a class-conscious, illustrated magazine which opposed the view of bourgeois mass-media publications. Among the contributors to this magazine was John Heartfield, famous for his new style of photomontages. In Hungary, the magazine *Erdekes Ussag* was an early example of modern photojournalism. In 1923, the *Münchner Illustrierte Presse* was first published, in a conscious imitation of the successful *Berliner Illustrirte*; both these publications soon reached a circulation of half a million. Unlike the bourgeois magazines, *AIZ* carried hardly any advertisements. It was not produced in free competition but by the party organization, which also guaranteed any deficit. New publications were not long in following: *Die Kölnische Illustrierte*, *Hackebeil's Illustrierte* (later known as *Die Neue Illustrierte*), *Die Hamburger Illustrierte*, and the *Feuerreiter* (which was financed by Catholic organizations). Other magazines were *Die Stuttgarter Illustrierte*, *Das Illustrierte Blatt* (Frankfurt), *Die Deutsche Illustrierte*, *Die Republikanische Illustrierte*, and a number of smaller publications. The National Socialists brought out

Der Illustrierte Beobachter which, like the *AIZ,* was financed by a political party.

There were also a number of illustrated weekly supplements to newspapers on a high level of quality: *Das Berliner Tageblatt (Weltspiegel)*, *Die Vossische Zeitung (Zeitspiegel)*, and the *Börsenkurier*. In addition, there were *Das Magazin* (edited at times by Stefan Lorant) and *Sport im Bild*, edited by Erich Maria Remarque. The Ullstein publishers put out the monthly magazines *Die Dame*, *Uhu*, and *Querschnitt* which, in addition to the written copy, placed emphasis on outstanding photographs. The monthly journal, *Atlantis*, first published in 1929, edited by the exceptionally sensitive and perceptive "photo-conservative" Martin Hürlimann, was devoted mainly to photographs on travel and foreign lands and peoples, publishing reportage-like photoessays on these themes.

The *Berliner Illustrirte* continued to lead the field in circulation, number of pages, and advertisements, due chiefly to its serial novels directed toward the middle-class reader. The leading writer was Vicki Baum, probably the most successful author of the twenties, if we disregard Remarque's *All Quiet on the Western Front*. Her entertaining novels written for the *Berliner Illustrirte* were of a high literary standard and were originally conceived as serials. Her *Grand Hotel*, inspired by the last public appearance of the ballerina Anna Pavlova, achieved worldwide success both in book form and as a film starring Greta Garbo and John and Lionel Barrymore.

Among the artists acquired by Kurt Korff for the Ullstein firm were Hans Baluschek, the portrayer of the proletarian way of life who later transferred to the *Arbeiter Illustrierte*; the easy-going Fritz Koch-Gotha; the amusing and satirical Lionel Feininger, who was later to become world-famous as a modern painter; the witty and ironic Walter Trier and Paul Simmel; and the brilliant and lordly Theo Matejko, a born "reporter-with-pencil," whose portrayals of races were as gripping as those of legal proceedings. It was Korff, in collaboration with Carl Schnebel, who first used a full-page photograph as an eye-catching cover picture—an idea which was soon copied by all the other magazines. The *AIZ,* the *Kölnische Illustrierte*, and the *Feuerreiter* were all printed in photogravure. Although the *Berliner Illustrirte* and other magazines appeared with a white frame around the cover picture for technical reasons, the *AIZ*, London's *Illustrated* and *Picture Post* and New York's *Life* and *Look* were able to fill the entire page with a picture.

Korff, of the *Berliner Illustrirte*, was always on the lookout for new talents—both writers and photographers. In the twenties he also sought out photoreporters capable of portraying a theme with strong human interest. But photoreporters of this kind did not appear until 1928–9, and it was not Korff who discovered them, except for Erich Salomon. They emerged on their own, very few coming from the ranks of the professional photographer.

The modern photoreporter was the creator of the modern illustrated magazine and modern photojournalism—not the other way round. The editors-in-chief of the magazines recognized his importance for photojournalism and they quickly welcomed him with open arms, incorporating him into the format of the modern illustrated magazine.

The pictorial sections of the magazines remained static during these years. A forward movement came, finally, from two sources, one expected and one totally unexpected. The first source was the continuing development of the camera and the lens. The second, entirely unforeseen, came about through the emergence of a small group of intellectual outsiders from this hitherto "unintellectual" field of press photography.

Camera progress meant achieving a handier format. Lenses developed for these smaller cameras had a greater depth of field; the Ernostar lens being capable of a greater light sensitivity. Film of no less than thirty-six exposures was advanced quickly in less than a second per frame, which also eliminated the possibility of double exposures. The film was much more sensitive, and this, combined with the other developments, resulted in a decisive simplification of exposure technique.

The Leica originated as a by-product. Dr. Oskar Barnack made movie cameras for the firm of Leitz in Wetzlar. These cameras were used chiefly for shooting newsreels. Dr. Barnack developed a small, handy miniature camera to take the place of the exposure meter which had up until then been unreliable. Barnack constructed a focal-plane shutter with a single shutter speed of 1/40th of a second for this exposure meter camera (the exposure usual for movie cameras at the time). In the darkroom, an open roll of movie film two yards long was inserted into this miniature camera, and before a scene was shot with the large movie camera, the cameraman was able to take numerous shots with varying apertures using Barnack's miniature exposure meter camera (the lighting conditions remained the same). The roll of film was developed and fixed immediately and discarded only when the best possible aperture had been established. Each individual negative on this roll of film was the same size as the film used by the movie camera, i.e., 24 × 18 mm. In the interests of simplicity and rapidity, Barnack coupled the focal-plane shutter with the film advance system, in the same way they were coupled in the movie camera. Thus the possibility of double exposure was eliminated, and the film advance was automatic and assured. The lens was telescopically adjustable. With these elements, the basic principle of the modern small-format camera was born. But the first experiments proved that the grain of the film was too coarse to allow enlargement. Barnack decided to double the size of the single movie frame (24 × 18 mm) for his new camera, which resulted in a picture of 24 × 36 mm. The idea of the direct viewfinder, through which the photographer sees the world as through a clear window, was also Barnack's.

Thus it was that in 1913 the Leica was born—the first modern small-format camera making possible the creation of visual reports on the world around us in a technically uncomplicated, integrated process. It was not long before it became possible to take a series of thirty-six pictures on one film. Observation–experience–report approached each other more closely than had been dreamed of. The necessary concentration evolved from the perceived moment coupled with the technical capabilities of the camera. The Leica made it possible to produce images of hitherto unknown spontaneity.

Barnack constructed only two models at first. He made a series of trial pictures with his own camera, one of which shows a street scene during the military mobilization in 1914—already a "typical Leica photo" and a typical reportage photo taken with the modern 35 mm camera. Most of today's cameras are 35 mm cameras which use film with thirty-six frames. Despite the many improvements which have been made in Germany, Japan, and Switzerland, Barnack's basic principles have not been supplanted. With his invention, it became possible to capture and preserve natural and unfalsified moments of life with the degree of success, dependent only on the ability and temperament of the photographer. The lens became an extension and adjunct of the eye.

Further development of the Leica was interrupted by the outbreak of hostilities. After the war, Barnack constructed another metal cassette for the thirty-six-frame film to protect it from light and to accelerate changing the film. He also developed a covered focal-plane shutter for varying widths, which resulted in exposures ranging from 1/20th to 1/500th of a second. He also added a rangefinder focusing device which made it possible to set the correct distance by manual rotation of the lens.

During this time, Dr. Max Berek developed an excellent anastigmatic lens with a maximum aperture of 1:3.5. In 1924, the first six Leica cameras left the Leitz factory, the small number being a cautious calculation.

In the same year, another sensational camera came onto the market, the now legendary Ermanox 4 1/2 × 6 cm, produced by the firm of Ernemann in Dresden. The advanced element of this camera was the lens, for the Ernostar had a light sensitivity of 1:2 (later even 1:1.8), thus it was the fastest lens in the world. As stated in the first reports, it was possible to photograph human subjects indoors in normal electric light without the aid of flash, with an exposure of only half a second. This was made possible by the use of plates of a sensitivity of approximately 27 to 28 degrees Scheiner, i.e., around 17 DIN. The disadvantage of the Ermanox was that it was a plate camera with a ground glass focusing system, although the distances in meters were in fact marked, and it was possible to align the focus through the sportstyle viewfinder. The distance was then estimated or measured by a Leica rangefinder. It was necessary to remove the plate after each exposure and insert a new one, and it was only possible to take indoor pictures with the aid of a tripod. Outdoors, under better lighting conditions, the Ermanox was, in fact, superfluous and also too complicated to handle; the Nettel Contessa 6 × 9 plate camera was superior.

Actually both the Leica and the Ermanox were sensational only in an historical sense and for the few reporters who recognized their value at the time. From 1924 to 1930, they were chiefly regarded as little more than amusing playthings.

In 1925, a physician, Dr. Paul Wolff, bought a Leica camera and enthusiastically began experimenting with various films and developers with a view to overcoming the coarse grain of the small-format film. His experiments were successful, and he gave up medicine to become a professional photographer. Together with a friend, Alfred Tritschler, he established a very successful photo studio for portraits, landscapes, and industrial advertising pictures in Frankfurt. He also created cover photos for magazines, all taken with Leica cameras. Most of his pictures were posed and had a pleasing quality. However, Wolff's greatest contribution to photography was that he demonstrated, as early as 1928, that the Leica was a worthy competitor of the larger format camera. A lack of absolute fineness in the grain of his enlargements was compensated for by the realistic surface texture.

The Leica and the Ermanox were both born reporter cameras. All that was missing were born photoreporters. Almost without exception, these first appeared on the scene in 1928 and 1929.

IV. The Development of Modern Photoreportage

In 1928, Kurt Korff was the editor-in-chief of the *Berliner Illustrirte Zeitung*. The publishing director was Kurt Szafranski, responsible also for the monthly magazines *Die Dame* and *Uhu*. Carl Schnebel was art director.

At the *Münchner Illustrierte Presse* the publishing director and moving spirit in the modernization of the magazine was Pflaum. Paul Feinhals was the sensitive and artistic editor-in-chief. Hugo Huber was in charge of the layout.

The *Berliner Illustrirte* (which, like the *Leipziger Illustrirte,* omitted the *e* in the word *Illustrierte*) was distinguished by the quality of its presentation, its fine photographs, and above all, the interesting serials by successful writers. In 1928, it also published short stories and essays by Kurt Tucholsky, Carl Zuckmayer, Arnold Zweig, and Bertolt Brecht. It presented many innovations which were hitherto unknown in the illustrated magazines—an excellent report on a legal proceeding, with text and drawings by Theo Matejko, and a number of reportages by the English travel writer and photographer James Abbé. There were Bengt Berg's excellent nature photographs of sea swallows and peregrine falcons covering two to three pages, and Thomas Mann's essay on photography, "The World is Beautiful," which was published as an appendix to a book of photographs by Renger-Patzsch. One of the new names was that of the freelance photographer Wolfgang Weber, whose sensational article "Foreign Industry on the Battlefields" was illustrated with photographs.

The *Münchner Illustrierte Presse*, on the other hand, was somewhat provincial, failing to provide any imaginative innovations in this year. It did, however, present a series of informative, illustrated political articles on themes such as disarmament, the League of Nations, the United States, and Soviet Russia. Wolfgang Weber also contributed a reportage to the *MIP*, this time on the theme of streets in big cities—a sociological report based on photographs taken by himself and others. A report on the sensational start of the Zeppelin in America appeared in another issue, accompanied by a few uninteresting group pictures ("Smile please! Now!") of Eckener and others present at the occasion. But, like the *BIZ*, the cover picture was always a large-format "eye-catcher."

The year 1928 also saw the beginning of the competitive battle between the *MIP* and the *BIZ* for larger circulation figures, and thus for a larger income from advertising. Generally speaking, the production costs of an illustrated magazine were approximately ten per cent higher than the income, and it was only advertisements which brought any profit. The larger the circulation, the higher was the advertising rate and the greater the profit.

The *Berliner Illustrirte* had at the time a circulation of around 1,600,000; the *Münchner Illustrierte* slightly less than 500,000. The Berlin magazine was fortunate to have on its staff a new photographer, Erich Salomon. His pictures completely changed the character of indoor reports, and his work was published mainly in the *BIZ*, *Die Dame*, and also the *Münchner Illustrierte*. As at the takeoff of the Zeppelin or at conferences, the participants hitherto had been obliged to form a group in the open air, or at best around the conference table. They gazed (as is largely the case today on television) into the camera with a pleasant expression, and the picture would be taken. Now, however, completely unposed and undirected interior photographs of entirely unselfconscious subjects began to appear in the magazines. Salomon, in a dinner jacket or tails and white tie, was a part of the occasion. He conversed with ministers and diplomats in German, French, or English, and he was familiar with the problems under discussion. Wherever he went, he took his camera, an Ermanox, and placed it on a tripod somewhere in the room, sometimes concealed in a hat, sometimes in a leather bag. People trusted Salomon and his camera; he disturbed no one, and thus no one disturbed him. Salomon often stood twelve, fifteen, or eighteen feet away from his camera. This was his psychological trick, or, to describe it better, his technical-psychological method. He held the long trigger cable unnoticed in his hand, quietly observed the scene, and when the moment came, simply released the shutter.

Salomon's exposures were between one-fifth of a second and a second. He concentrated intuitively and intensely on the decisive moment, which at the same time was the moment of relaxation in a conversation and in the accompanying gestures and expressions. Almost always a relatively brief period, the mood would build to a point at which four or five persons would be listening to the speaker with intense concentration. It was at such a moment that Salomon would release the shutter and keep it open until a split second before the tension ended. He sensed this split second instinctively and was able to wait. To avoid disturbing the moment by the sound of the focal-plane shutter, Salomon often used the quiet Compur shutter which he had placed in front of the lens. Thus with the focal-plane shutter open, he operated only this Compur shutter. His subjects were aware that they were being photographed, but they did not know just when. And as Salomon was skilled in changing the plate without attracting attention, the "great ones" were usually surprised when Salomon showed them the pictures.

In a single picture, Salomon was able to capture the mood of the speaker, the listeners, and the whole group. He had respect for the truth of what he saw through the lens. He recognized the limits of his methods, but he made the fullest possible use of their potentialities. Salomon also took extremely impressive portraits of individuals. Here too his images reveal his conscious self-limitation.

He made but few picture series and few complete reportages. Most of his work consisted of reportage-like single pictures. The outdoor reportage did not interest him, and he restricted himself to the field in which he was a master: the indoor photoreportage in available light. He possessed an infallible intuition for the essential moment. Once when he was present at a dinner at the Royal Academy, an official tried to prevent him from taking photos by saying "That has never been done here!" Salomon's lofty reply was: "That's why I'm going to do it!"

Salomon used the Ermanox almost exclusively up until 1932, when he bought his first Leica and a 20 cm telelens. He was thus able to shoot his pictures from a considerable distance. He did not disturb his subjects, and they did not disturb him.

Salomon was first and foremost a photographer of political events. Once during the Munich October Festival, my brother and I collaborated with him. He took the pictures in the stalls, and we photographed the colorful outdoor scenes. Salomon's pictures caused a sensation throughout the world, and they appeared in many magazines in Europe, England, and America. It was then, in 1929, that the editor of the illustrated weekly *Graphic* coined the phrase "candid camera" for Salomon's photos—a phrase which was to become the keyword of a new type of reportage photos. Although not always unposed, such photos are always revealing, even when without socio-critical undertone.

The words "unposed" and "unobserved" have often been applied to this new and thoroughly contemporary style of photoreportage. However, they are not always used accurately. Every good photoreporter sometimes finds himself in the position of having to say "Don't let me disturb you!" or "Would you mind doing that again?" (for example, the action of throwing a sack of corn into the air). The good photoreporter is also a good documentary director. He never poses something which has not happened just for the sake of photographic impact. But it is quite valid to repeat a scene which actually took place.

Salomon took his first reportage pictures in the law courts during the famous Hein murder trial in Coburg. His Ermanox was concealed in a briefcase in which he had made a hole for the lens. From that day he became known as a star photographer. He had found his profession and his vocation.

His son reports that "Salomon now profited from the various talents and abilities which he had acquired over the years: worldly wisdom, a knowledge of languages, and charm. A passion for construction also made him inventive as when it came to concealing his cameras, and his legal training provided the criterion of just how much manipulation was consistent with true reportage. It was not long before he decided to pose his subjects only when circumstances made it inevitable."

In 1929, Salomon traveled to the United States to take photographs for the American newspaper king of the time, William Randolph Hearst. Hearst was so enthusiastic about the results that he had an Ermanox sent over from Germany for each of his photographers; there were almost fifty. The trouble was that he forgot to order fifty Salomons. He was badly disappointed when his fifty reporters and their fifty new Ermanox cameras turned out to be fifty failures!

Though he maintained that he was fully justified in taking pictures of people in the public interest, Salomon abhorred any entry into private lives. This respect for the private life of the individual as well as that of the public personality came naturally to all the photoreporters of the day. Today's photographic "snooper," as portrayed by Fellini in his film *La Dolce Vita*—a kind of buzzing, stinging, and thoroughly unpleasant insect—is the blackmailing jackal of journalism.

It was not so much the unobserved moment but the moment of naturalness which the representatives of the new photojournalism seized. As with every photoreporter "worthy of his camera," the subject not only *acts* naturally in his presence, he *is* natural. Salomon was never a disturbing element, and his Ermanox seemed to be a part of him. In his field, and considering the limitations of his equipment, he is the undisputed master of our century. The first "unlimited" camera was the Leica, the camera of other photoreporters of the time.

Salomon published his first photographs in the *Berliner Illustrirte* and the *Münchner Illustrierte*, and the latter magazine decided to enter into serious competition with the Berlin journal.

The new editor in Berlin for the *Münchner Illustrierte* was the young Stefan Lorant, then editor of the *Filmkurier*, the Sunday supplement to the *Berliner Börsenkurier*. Lorant had previously attempted to instill a new vigor into the style and content of the *Münchner Illustrierte*, and in September 1928, the paper published a reportage in pictures and text covering several pages entitled "The Chanson Reflects Our Time" with photos of Fritzi Massary, Claire Waldoff, and other typical Berlin cabaret personalities. Such representative themes and their manner of presentation lent the *Münchner Illustrierte* a cosmopolitan accent and courted readership in northern Germany and Berlin.

Lorant went to Vienna from Budapest at the age of twenty as a photographer of so-called stills, film scenes posed for advertising purposes. It was not long before he became a cameraman for the film *The Life, Loves, and Sorrows of Mozart*; he also wrote the script and directed the film *Love's Fool*. (His own comment on this film: "It was a major disaster!")

From Vienna Lorant moved to Berlin where he was first employed as second cameraman for the successful film *The Count of Essex*. In 1925, however, he gave up his career as a film cameraman and began writing newspaper articles, one of which, "Behind the Scenes of the Haller Revue," published in the journal *Das Magazin,* December 1925, lists Stefan Lorant as author of text and pictures and includes the note that "all the pictures were taken with an Ernemann Ermanox." In August 1928 he was promoted to Berlin editor of the *Münchner Illustrierte*. Because all photoagencies were in Berlin, and as a result of its new cosmopolitan policy, the Munich paper's Berlin editorship was of equal status with that in Munich. Thus the contributions from the Berlin offices frequently surpassed those of Munich. The opposite temperaments of Lorant and Feinhals often led to underground rivalry which considerably complicated the collaboration for which Pflaum had hoped. "We were always getting in each other's hair," says Lorant. "We were both young, ambitious, and stubborn, and we had basically different conceptions of editorship." Lorant was editor-in-chief for a time in 1929, only to be succeeded by Feinhals. But the main burden of the picture responsibility shifted to Lorant in Berlin, for he had displayed an alert sense for latent topical themes.

When suggestions were brought to him by agencies or photoreporters, he recognized their topical potentialities and he organized the suitable graphic presentation for publication. He underlined the "essay" character of the photoreportage and identified himself with the photos as if they were his own. He emphasized graphic presentation and arrangement instead of showing a mere succession of photos, text, and captions. Even if the *Berliner Illustrirte* published reportages which were just as good if not better than those in the *Münchner Illustrierte,* their presentation was too strongly stamped with the graphic style of Kurt Korff and Carl Schnebel. The breakthrough to modern, lively presentation did not take place until the *Münchner Illustrirte* came under Lorant's influence.

At the end of 1930, Feinhals joined the *Kölnische Illustrierte* which soon became Germany's third "great" magazine under his skilful direction. Always a sensitive artist, Feinhals—together with Korff and Lorant—brought new life to photojournalism. The *Münchner Illustrierte* then became the responsibility of its art director, Hugo Huber—Lorant had an Hungarian passport—although in practice, if not in name, Lorant functioned as editor-in-chief. In 1932, however, as the magazine became more and more successful, he did in fact assume the position. The relationship of mutual trust between Lorant and the photographers permitted them to treat their themes as they thought fit. The photographers could always be confident that Lorant's presentations would display their work to best advantage. They knew also that Lorant would not accept mediocre work. There were no permanently employed photographers, and thus every photoreportage accepted was a new proof of the photoreporter's ability. This mutual dependence between photoreporter and editor may explain why Lorant was seldom obliged to reject the work submitted and also why his photographers did not suffer the depressing disappointments which plagued American staff photographers in later years.

With the delivery of the pictures, the photoreporter's task was completed. Lorant made the selection and sketched the layout according to his own views—not according to those of the publishing directors. This gave the *Münchner Illustrierte* a distinctive, recognizable character, contributing greatly to its success. The so-called artistic style of presentation became increasingly rare, imaginative cropping and embellishments even rarer. The pictures were published in as natural, simple, and unfalsified a form as possible.

Another graphic principle was the reduction and limitation of the pictures to a double-page spread. The key photo was shown large, the rest intentionally smaller and grouped in harmonious sequence. Later, at the *Picture Post* particularly, Lorant developed the tendency further, and was aided in this by the photogravure printing process. The formal focal point of the individual pictures often resulted in an unobtrusive oval which related to the central idea and the graphic central point.

Competition which now arose among the growing number of German magazines led to an increase in fees offered to the photographers. The *Berliner Illustrirte* and the *Münchner Illustrierte* paid three hundred marks or more per page. *Die Woche* and *Die Kölnische* followed suit, but more modestly.

The increasing demand for publishable photos and reports led to the foundation, at the end of 1928, of two new photoagencies, Dephot (German Photo Service) and Weltrundschau. Unlike the existing agencies (particularly Keystone, Pacific and Atlantic Press Association, Wide World, A.B.C., and Hanke) they dealt with the programming and production of photoreportages as well as distribution. The cofounder and director of Dephot was Simon Gutmann, and Weltrundschau was directed from 1928 on by Rudolph Birnbach, a Rumanian by birth. They were in constant contact with the editors and the staff reporters of magazines and newspapers, and their work consisted of composing, perfecting, and placing photoreportages. Their stimulating influence on both editors and reporters was considerable. This was true on a smaller scale of the Hungarian-born Henry Guttmann, who lived in Paris and Berlin and worked mainly with two photoreporters, E. P. Hahn-Gilland from

Frankfurt and André Kertesz in Paris. Guttmann's special interest was to collect old photographs and put them together with a text to form a picture story. He rediscovered many long-forgotten photos from the 19th century. In 1930, he wrote the first comprehensive work on the early days of photography, for which Helmut Theodor Bossert contributed the foreword.

Following the Dephot's and Weltrundschau's example, Keystone and Associated Press (under the direction of Leon Daniel) decided in 1930 to embark on their own production of photoreportages in addition to their distribution of single pictures. Pacific and Atlantic was already known as a distributor of picture reports from all over the world, and was taken over by Associated Press.

The backbone of the new photojournalism, however, was still the individual photoreporter. In 1929 came the breakthrough of photoreportage conceived as a complete and harmonious whole, which represented the beginning of modern photojournalism. These reportages, often planned on a psychological basis and attractively presented, were immediately recognized by the magazines and their readers as the best and most appealing form of the photographic report. In only a few short months new men came into the field, independent of one another and often unaware of the others' existence. Together with Salomon, these new men were to create modern photoreportage.

The year 1929 began with a photojournalistic sensation. In the first issue of the *Berliner Illustrirte,* three pages were devoted to "The House of Silence," a series of pictures on the Motherhouse of the Trappist order, Notre-Dame de la Grande Trappe, in Soligny. It was unusual to devote three pages to a single theme, but in this case it was thoroughly justified. The unposed photographs by the Paris photographer André Kertesz showed scenes, never before made public, of the daily lives of the Trappists in their secluded monastery of silence. There were pictures of the monks in their cells and on their way to mass, at table, and at a vigil by an open coffin. The powerful photos had an impact which brought the monks as human beings closer to the reader. The reportage did more than present a visual image of the subject. It transported the viewer into the atmosphere of the monastery, conveying vividly not only the environment, but also the monks' feelings and way of life.

André Kertesz was a poetic photographer who produced few comprehensive picture series. His story on the life of the Trappists, however, is one of the most impressive reportages ever created. Kertesz was filled with insatiable human curiosity—an essential characteristic of the true photoreporter. Occasionally this characteristic can have the disadvantage of producing a statement too subjective in a situation calling for more objective treatment. But for Kertesz this danger did not exist. Brassaï once wrote: "When I met André Kertesz, I was captivated by the medium of photography." Cartier-Bresson recognized him as his model and teacher in much the same way.

The cover of the year's first issue of the *Berliner Illustrirte* was a photo by the theater photographer Freiherr von Gudenberg taken with an Ermanox. It showed Richard Strauss conducting an opera performance—a picture in the best "Salomon style," powerfully evoking the atmosphere of the moment in which it was taken. (The previous pioneer of unposed stage pictures was Hans Böhm who had been photographing in Vienna since 1925.)

After the first issue of 1929, the *Berliner Illustrirte* only published very few photoreportages of distinction. Its design had an element of uncertainty and was below its previous level. The initial strength with which the *BIZ* had begun the year was taken up and carried further by the *Münchner Illustrierte.*

The first 1929 issue of *MIP* contained a retrospective reportage on the Spartacus League struggles of 1919; in the fourth issue Wolfgang Weber published an illustrated report on the American worker. Number five contained a reportage on the Munich Carnival by Salomon which ran on two pages and the cover, a contribution which lacked vitality and color. Salomon had taken the photos at the suggestion of Lorant, but gripping reportages were not his métier. In contrast, page 157 showed Salomon's remarkable picture of "photographed music," taken in a dance hall with an exposure of three seconds; it anticipated "blurred photography" which was to become the fashion two decades later. The image of carnival dancing is full of life and movement because of the blurred effect.

In issue number six, two and one half more pages of Salomon's carnival pictures appeared, while number eleven contained a reportage by Salomon of a visit to Richard Strauss which appeared both on the cover and inside. A photo of Pablo Casals playing Bach, in number twelve, was to become a classic, and in the same issue E.P. Hahn-Gilland published "A Reportage without Light: A Night on the Beat," a series of impressive pictures of a policeman's beat.

New men came forward in rapid succession. The twenty-third issue of *MIP* offered "Servus Kumpel" by Ignaz Gidalewitsch (my civil name at the time), a report which showed a meeting of hippies in a wood near Stuttgart. Number twenty-seven had the first photoreportage by Georg Gidal, "Eight-hour Lecture," a series of pictures taken in secret during a lecture by the famous professor of anatomy Siegfried Mollier. Number twenty-eight presented "Swimming Pool in Lunapark," photographed by Hans Baumann but published under the name of Dephot.

The large number of photoreportages which appeared in the *Münchner Illustrierte* in 1929 included the following: "Parisian Country Dances" by E. P. Hahn-Gilland; "International Politics in The Hague" ("Our colleague Kelen has now turned his attention to psychological photography in addition to his activities as a draftsman" ran the subtitle —the first time that the word "psychological" was applied to this new kind of photoreportage); "The Moritat as an Opera" by I. and G. Gidal, a picture report on *The Threepenny Opera*, taken during a performance; "Paris Ghetto" by E. P. Hahn-Gilland; "Between Midnight and Dawn on the Kurfürstendamm" by Dephot-Man (the name assumed by Hans Baumann); "Auto Racing on the Nürburgring" by Dephot-Man; "George Bernard Shaw, Emperor of America," a theater reportage by Salomon and Man; "The Juggler Rastelli" by Umbo; "The Private Life of Karl Valentin" by Tim Gidal; "The European Boxing Championship" by Schneid and Man; "Child and Kasperl" by Georg Gidal; "Small Town Life" by Wolfgang Weber; "Adoption Agency" by Umbo; "Pawnshop" by Wolfgang Weber; "Circus Town" by Georg Gidal. Many more reportages by these men appeared in the *Münchner Illustrierte* in the same year. Other magazines published numerous photoreportages also, and by a widening number of photoreporters including Neudin (Weltrundschau), Walter Bosshard, and Seldow (Weltrundschau). Weber, Umbo, Man, and the Gidal brothers published additional work in other journals during this year. Weber, Bosshard, and the Gidals always worked alone and usually wrote their own texts. Salomon would submit only the names of his subjects with his pictures. Other photoreporters of the time worked in collaboration with journalists who planned the reportage and wrote the text.

In 1929, photoreportage, via the *Münchner Illustrierte*, took the decisive step toward becoming a clearly defined, generally accepted branch of journalism; and this was true also of photojournalism as a whole. Although the years 1929 and 1930 were a period of stagnation for the *Berliner Illustrirte*, Szafranski and Korff were nevertheless engaged in preparing large-scale projects in order to catch up with the *Münchner*, the circulation of which had increased to a remarkable degree.

Other illustrated magazines quickly adopted the new medium of photoreportage, notably the *Kölnische Illustrierte* and the conservative *Feuerreiter*. *Atlantis*, *Die Dame*, and *Uhu* likewise included a number of photoreportages in their issues. Now finally and irrevocably, photoreportage had separated from art photography on the one hand and, on the other, from the influence of the new photographic artists such as Laszlo Moholy-Nagy, Baumeister, and Werner Gräff. Artificially produced effects subjectively manipulated during exposure and in the darkroom were now completely taboo for the photoreporter. The technical aspect was neither elevated nor degraded—it was regarded simply as what it was: the means to an end.

The preceeding titles bear witness to the fact that the main theme of photoreportage was the everyday life of all kinds of people. Beautiful or ugly, positive or negative in mood —the human attitude of the photoreporter, an honest report of what he saw and felt, became the determining criterion. By this direct method of reportage, the reader came to experience previously unnoticed aspects of life and was enabled to participate in a reality which the photoreporter saw. Five million purchasers of German illustrated magazines in 1930 meant at least twenty million actual readers—about half the German population over ten years of age. The world, or sections of it, was made accessible by this visual means of mass communications. The population was "in the picture."

Whereas the serial novels published in the illustrated magazines represented, for the most part, a form of escapism for millions of readers—escapism to an illusory dream world—the photoreportages were less illusory, unlike today's magazines with their preprogrammed picture series. The escape to a better illusion can sometimes be a legitimate substitute and can help to correct social conditions, although only in the realm of fantasy. On the other hand, it also tends to maintain inadequate social conditions. Thus it was, from a sociological point of view, that the serial stories had a soporific effect, whereas the photoreportages often had an instructive and thought-provoking impact. In spite of this, it is true nevertheless that such photoreportages—to quote the American photographer Hine (1910)—tended merely to show conditions as they were rather than to provide any suggestion of how they might be improved.

The Leica and Ermanox were joined in 1929–30 by two new medium-sized reporter cameras: the twin-lens reflex camera Rolleiflex f: 3.5, and the extremely handy folding Plaubel Makina f: 2.9. The Rolleiflex was produced in two sizes for negatives of 4 × 4 cm and 6 × 6 cm. Both cameras are still on the market, and both take films of twelve frames. The Plaubel Makina was only about two inches thick when folded, and it was possible to use a film pack cassette with twelve sheet films instead of plates.

Bosshard, the Gidal brothers, Neudin, and Weber started by using the Leica and, for special purposes, the Ermanox, Rolleiflex, and Plaubel Makina. Kertesz used the Leica in 1928, Munkacsi worked with a 9 × 12 cm reflex camera, and later (from 1931) with a Rolleiflex and a Leica. Man (Hans Baumann) used a Nettel Contessa plate camera with 6½ × 9 cm plates and (from the end of 1929) an Ermanox. His interior exposure times were a quarter to half a second, and this often resulted in underexposure which he then compensated for by using uranium intensifier.

In 1932, he changed over to the Leica, which was in fact the best all-around reporter camera. Whereas his work had consisted hitherto of interior photographs, largely taken with the use of a tripod—from this point on more and more of his photos were made for outdoor reportages.

Kurt Hübschmann (later known as Kurt Hutton) also used an Ermanox (from 1929) and (from 1930) a Leica too. Alfred Eisenstaedt used a variety of cameras, including the Ermanox: "I decided that I needed an Ermanox if I was going to produce pictures like Salomon's." In 1931, he bought a Leica. The influence of the Ermanox and the Leica on these early reporters was undeniably great.

Walter Bosshard published photos in reportage style as early as 1929 in the *Illustrated London News* and in *Atlantis* – pictures of an expedition to Central Asia. From 1930, Dephot distributed his work. Bosshard's outstanding talent as a photoreporter was recognized immediately upon publication of his first pictures, a verdict confirmed by his subsequent success.

Originally Wolfgang Weber was a student of musicology. My brother Georg Gidal had studied biology. Neudin, after making acquaintance with the Leica, interrupted his studies in architecture. I myself had studied history and art history, and Man was a sports illustrator for *BZ am Mittag*. Like Salomon, we emerging photoreporters came to the new medium by chance more or less. And the laws of chance should not be underestimated in this case.

Man's first series of pictures, "Swimming Pool in Lunapark," was distinguished by its unforced vigor and liveliness—a fact all the more surprising when we consider that he used a Nettel Contessa camera mounted on a tripod (this was one of the most usual sports cameras at the time). For this series Man used a model who appears in five of the eight pictures published. Three months later, his reportage "Between Midnight and Dawn on the Kurfürstendamm" was published. This series revealed him as an alert observer and outstanding technician successful in capturing the night scene despite the indispensable tripod. Man's most outstanding achievement was a five-page reportage, "A Day with Mussolini," which appeared in the *Münchner Illustrierte Presse* (No. 9, 1931). It was distinguished above all by the interior photos taken in available light.

In one of the pictures, taken in a huge and magnificent room in the Palazzo Chigi, Mussolini looks like a dummy and out of place, stocky and awkward, talking to the Rome correspondent of the *Münchner Illustrierte*. This born orator radiated an uncanny fascination when speaking to the masses. Here, however, he shows an element of the tragicomical; he was known in England as the "Sawdust Caesar." The "marble pillars" and "woodcarvings" in the huge hall were anything but genuine; like an additional piece of irony, they were simply painted on the walls.

In 1929, Felix H. Man joined Dephot as production director for photojournalism. The one-time Bauhaus student Umbo (Otto Umbehr) also belonged to Dephot; Lorant called him a "Jack-of-all-trades, the most versatile man in the group—there was nothing he could not do."

Hübschmann started out with Dephot, then joined Weltrundschau for a time. His pictures radiate a sympathy for the human beings whom he described by means of photography. Neudin, whose real name was Neudatschin, was staff reporter for Weltrundschau. A native of the Baltic region, he was a typical "frantic reporter." "For a reporter nothing is impossible," was his opinion, and he succeeded in getting reportages behind prison walls, in brothels, and of secret military exercises. He did a lot of work for the *Berliner Illustrirte* and the *Kölnische*. He built facilities in his car which included a miniature darkroom and a well-equipped food locker. Other contributors to Weltrundschau included Belkin, Seldow, and Comeriner.

My brother and I, like Wolfgang Weber, Salomon, and others, were not committed to any one agency. Nevertheless, we submitted several series to Weltrundschau for primary distribution, and almost all our work for secondary distribution. Weltrundschau had good connections to illustrated magazines in Germany as well as to branches in France, Holland, Switzerland, Belgium, and Scandinavia. Our loose relationship with Weltrundschau had the advantage of allowing us to choose our themes—except for Lorant's commissions. In addition, we were not tied to a schedule. We alternated between study semesters and periods of working as photoreporters. My brother Georg had been an excellent amateur photographer for many years and had illustrated a number of essays on arts and crafts with his own photos. Already at the age of thirteen, he was able to print his pictures on daylight paper which he laid on the negative plate in a wooden frame in the darkened bathroom, pressed against the negative by means of a folding wooden plate and a press. He then exposed the plate and the paper to sunlight for a short time, removed the daylight paper from the frame in the darkroom, carefully fixed it under a yellow safe light, and washed it for a certain period. My role during this nerve-racking procedure was limited to that of a passive onlooker. When the exposure was correct and the picture appeared in sufficient contrast and detail, it would be greeted by a cry of triumph; if not, a resigned "No good this time" would ensue. Later, as I was studying art history with professors Pinder and Wölfflin, I learned many synonyms for these reactions, but my brother's laconic remarks have remained my most impressive acquaintance with expressions of success or failure.

I myself first entered the field of photoreportage through Fritz Goro, a friend who was then a talent scout and contact man for the *Münchner Illustrierte*. The reportage "Servus Kumpel" was well received and led to further commissions. I encouraged my brother to make photoreportages of his own with the idea that if we each created one reportage a month, we could continue our studies wherever we chose. He borrowed a Leica from our older brother (also an amateur photographer) and secretly took pictures in a classroom during a lecture by the great anatomist Mollier, with whom he was studying. The professor lecturing, the students with concentrated expressions, and the skeleton which gave rise to philosophical reflection, all combined to make a well-balanced, atmospheric reportage. The series appeared on two pages, and my brother thus became a photoreporter. Unlike my first attempts at photoreportage, every one of his pictures was "just right" and technically flawless.

From then on we did not limit ourselves to one reportage per month. We had become passionate photoreporters and published numerous reportages accompanied by our own texts in the *Münchner*, the *Berliner*, the *Kölner*, and other magazines. From 1930 on, Georg Gidal did a great deal of work for Arnold Kübler's *Zürcher*, in which he introduced the modern German photoreportage to Switzerland. Kübler was both an understanding and stimulating employer; the conservatism of the *Zürcher Illustrierte* was soon altered under his guidance. Occasionally he would publish photoreportages four or five pages long, and some of them were subsequently used by the *Münchner* and the *Berliner*.

My brother Georg was fatally injured in an automobile accident while traveling on an assignment in the autumn of 1931. We had worked on many reportages together. One day we saw a picture of the Berlin premiere of *The Threepenny Opera* in the *Berliner Illustrirte*. Taken during the dress rehearsal, it showed Mack the Knife standing happily beneath the gallows, looking soulfully and cheerfully upward. We decided to try a reportage on *The Threepenny Opera* during the Munich premiere, which we felt would be more atmospheric. My brother used an Ermanox, I a Leica. We had a problem since at that time the 35 mm film did not have the high sensitivity of the plates and the widest aperture was only f:3.5, as opposed to the Ernostar which had a light sensitivity of f:2, later of f:1.8 even. To solve this problem I constructed a chain stand, one end of which I screwed into the base of the Leica. With one foot on the other end, I braced the chain, held my breath, and released the shutter. In this way I was able to take unblurred pictures even during poorly lit scenes with exposures of one fifth of a second or longer. I still use this method for interior photographs and with color film of low sensitivity.

While working on this reportage I discovered that there is always a split second of stillness before one movement is followed by another in a different direction. If one manages to perceive and arrest this split second (for example, in the case of conductors, dancers, speakers), it is possible to take unblurred photographs in available light. I now know that Hans Böhm had discovered and used this principle as early as 1927, and his photographs were unposed most of the time.

In 1930, the position of the *Münchner* as a place for new photoreporters became even stronger. It was to last another year before the *Berliner* finally adopted the new journalism, and apart from a few reportages by Neudin, Munkacsi, Georg Gidal and Kertesz, there was not much of the new spirit of reportage to be felt at the *Berliner*. It was as if its editorial staff were resting on old laurels, whereas most of the other magazines were publishing photoreportages from all fields.

Some of Munkacsi's photos showed scenes of the newly created Liberia. One picture portrays a mother with bared bosom dressed in national costume, fetching from school her son who is dressed in modern clothes—the end of one era and the beginning of another.

The *Münchner* published a number of reportages by Wolfgang Weber, Man, E. P. Hahn, Neudin, the Gidals, Salomon, Hübschmann, Umbo, and Bosshard. Other photoreporters made many unique contributions. An anonymous report on the Salvation Army by Pacific and Atlantic had a particularly strong effect. The following titles reveal the degree to which the modern photoreportage, in the second year of its existence, had taken its place as an integral part of photojournalism:

"Drought in France" by E. P. Hahn-Gilland; "The Nürburgring at Night" by Man; "Five Indian Reportages" by Bosshard; "Art School" by Umbo; "Hamburg's Transients" by Weber; "Arabs versus Jews—Palestine's Problem" by Tim Gidal; "Soccer—May in Auteuil" by E. P. Hahn-Gilland; "World Boxing Championship" submitted by an agency; "Poverty in Hamburg" by Neudin; "Pilgrimage to Altötting" by Weber; "Max Reinhardt's Acting School" by Man; "The Last Hand Weavers in the Glatzer Mountains" by Man; "Diving School" by Neudin; "Emigrants in Hamburg" by Neudin; "Goethe's House" by Hübschmann; "Rescue in a Gas-Filled Shaft" by Neudin; "Munich Television Station—German Museum" by Tim Gidal; "Today's Single Woman" by Man; "The Cathedral Sparrows of Regensburg" by Georg Gidal.

Strangely enough, in 1930, only one new name joined

those of 1928 and 1929 in the German illustrated magazines. Walter Bosshard's first reportage revealed unerring assurance and unruffled courage. He went on to create the most profound and far-reaching photoreportages of the international political scene throughout the 1930s.

The *Münchner Illustrierte* contracted Bosshard via Dephot for German publication of the pictures he took in India in 1930. Bosshard gained Gandhi's confidence and accompanied him on the famous "salt march," virtually the beginning of India's fight for independence from Great Britain. Bosshard's photos and text were published all over the world, arousing sympathy for India's struggle for independence.

The series of Bosshard's reports in the *Münchner Illustrierte* began with three pages entitled "India 1930," an informative reportage. The next contribution was a dramatic report on the "salt march." A few weeks later, the *Münchner* presented two pages with the theme: "50,000 Indians Defy the Salt Monopoly," with pictures of the resulting unrest and action by the British police. In the next issue, number twenty, a close-up of Gandhi reading a newspaper appeared on the cover with the title: "Mahatma Gandhi Reading: The Man Who Challenged the British Empire." The issue contained pictures which, in direct contrast to the mass demonstrations all over India, showed Gandhi shortly before his arrest in his home; Gandhi reading to his collaborators a satirical poem about himself from an English newspaper; Gandhi taking a nap on the floor; Gandhi eating onion soup. Three weeks later, a photo-and-text reportage by Bosshard presented the theme of "Boycott and Rebellion in India." The series closed with a strikingly pertinent and explanatory photostory covering three pages on the subject of "The Indian Village." Thus Bosshard, in no less than five consecutive reportages, had captured and illuminated the most important international event of 1930—the Gandhi movement—from various angles in pictures and text by a single reporter. The series was followed a few weeks later, as a postscript, by Bosshard's three-page report on "The India of the Maharajas."

Wolfgang Weber, from the beginning of his career, clearly was one of the authentic pioneers of modern photoreportage. After studying ethnology, he spent some time at the Munich Academy of Music with the aim of becoming an operatic conductor. In 1925, he organized a journey to Kilimanjaro where he recorded the songs of a Chagga tribe on wax cylinders—the predecessors of the tape recorder—for an institute of musicology. However, he was more interested in Africa's political situation, and he published articles illustrated by his own photos and postcards in the *Vossische Zeitung* and other publications. He first began taking pictures in 1923—stereo pictures for Papa Mücke's *Panorama* in Berlin, in which the images appeared in three-dimensional form.

It was probably a "wild" commission from Stefan Lorant which established Weber as a great but independent-minded photoreporter of sociological subjects. "The theme is The Citizen in Distress! Crisis in the Bavarian Forest! Go to the Bavarian border tonight, get all the information you possibly can on the protest meetings. The photos and text must be on my table the day after tomorrow!" A night's journey, a day's work, a night's return journey. The pictures were ready on time, but Weber and Lorant had a difference of opinion, and Lorant refused to accept the pictures. "I got into my car and drove through the night a third time, this time to Berlin, and the *Berliner* published the reportage in a multi-page spread and with a cover picture. I never wanted to see the *Münchner* again, and I decided to remain with the *Berliner*." This reportage was published in September 1931 with the title "Village Without Work." The cover picture had no title, but the caption "We don't want unemployment money or relief... we only want to work. On the land, on the roads—anywhere, anything!" said a lot. Five months later the *Münchner* published Weber's reportage "Deaf-and-Dumb School." Many more followed.

The Weber-Lorant episode was symptomatic of the independent status of the photoreporter at the beginning of modern photojournalism. It throws light on the working conditions which were in sharp contrast to later practices in the United States. There long discussions and detailed planning often preceded a reportage which then was the work of days, usually, rather than hours. This is largely still the case today. Although this kind of organization may have some advantages, the earlier reportages possessed a spontaneity and originality of communication which were unique. One of the virtues of the earlier method was probably the direct contact between editor and photoreporter. Today the approval of a department editor is no guarantee that the reportage will even be published.

The small number of established photoreporters in the late twenties and early thirties felt secure in their independence. Their relationships with the various editors were usually most friendly. Controversies did arise, of course: Neudin, for example, quarreled with Birnbach every three months approximately, and he had to be pacified by a parcel of food including smoked eel and champagne! Felix H. Man switched from the *Münchner* to the *Berliner* in 1932; Hübschmann left Dephot after a violent argument and worked for a time with Weltrundschau. I did the same, but my step was final. At any rate, it was an exciting and good period for us all.

Weber is still one of Germany's top reporters. He has published an eighty-page reportage on China in various magazines. Together with Madeleine Beck, his collaborator since 1955, he now makes documentary films for television.

In 1931, photoreportage finally was recognized by the *Berliner* as an important area of contemporary photojournalism. "There was an element of discontent (on the magazine) with the static photos," Szafranski recalls. "This is what led to experiments with new ideas, and thus the foundation for a new format for picture journalism was laid. The 'picture story,' as we now know it, was born." Although it is true to say that the foundation was laid by various German magazines, its success was due less to the *BIZ* than to the *Münchner Illustrierte Presse*, where its presentation also was so impressive.

The contribution of the *Berliner* before 1931 has been accurately described by its editor Kurt Korff: "The visual observation of events—coupled with a recognition of the greatest visual impact and the elimination of everything which was not of visual interest—became the basic principle of the *BIZ*."

Opposed to this view, however, were the single pictures of Salomon, the photoreporters of 1928 to 1933, and the *Münchner Illustrierte*—all of which emphasized the content of photoreportage. From this new emphasis, the new contemporary photoreportage was created. That it reached its culmination only in 1938–40, in the London magazine *Picture Post*, under Lorant, was due to a number of personal, intellectual, and economic factors.

Three important technical improvements contributed to the expansion of photoreportage in 1930. Agfa brought Agfa-Pan film onto the market. This film with ASA 32 (approximately 16 DIN) was equal to the sensitivity of plates. In 1931, Agfa Superpan (ASA 100) also became available, and from then on Agfa remained clearly ahead of Kodak and other competitors in the area of highly sensitive, fine-grain 35 mm film. The formula came to light only after the war when the ban on the publication of manufacturing secrets was lifted. It was the addition of gold (gold salts) that intensified both the sensitivity and grain fineness of the film.

In 1930, Leitz produced a Leica with interchangeable lenses—a wide-angle lens with a light intensity of f:3.5 and a focal length of 35 mm in place of the previous 50 mm; and a telephoto Elmar 1:4.5 and 135 mm. They also constructed a handier, attachable rangefinder. Osram produced a flash lamp which could be ignited with a flashlight battery. With the simplification of the technical aspects of photography, it became possible for the photoreporter to concentrate on the important essentials of the reportage.

New photoagencies were established in 1931. Most of these distributed the work of one or two photoreporters. The majority, however, were short-lived or restricted their activities to smaller publications. Only Alfred Eisenstaedt and Lechenperg attained the status of the "Old Guard." A few photographers, however, published outstanding single pictures in the style of Munkacsi and Kertesz. These were, mainly, Cami Stone, Seidenstücker, and Peter Weller. Eisenstaedt had already arrived on the scene with single pictures in reportage style.

One of the questions at the time was whether photographs could be printed in such a way that they would seem three-dimensional. That this process converted lively two-dimensional images into waxwork rigidity only became clear during subsequent experiments in 1950.

Stereoscopic apparatus for three-dimensional viewing of daguerreotypes had been produced as early as 1850. The stereoscope in the 1860s was an indispensable piece of the household equipment of every "proper" family in Germany, France, England, Switzerland, and, particularly, the United States. Series of stereoscopic pictures of far-away countries and of topical events were available on subscription. In Germany there were dealers who stocked more than 600,000 different photos, many of which were pornographic and erotic, most of these from France. In this context it is interesting to recall an article in the *Berliner Illustrirte* in 1931: "What Is the Best Way of Looking at Photographs?" The advice given for viewing three-dimensional pictures read as follows: "Close one eye and hold the photo at a distance of 5 to 7 inches (according to the size of the picture) until you see it in three dimensions." According to the rule that two minuses make a plus, this method would appear to be thoroughly effective.

During 1931, Bosshard was represented in the *Berliner* by reportages of Thailand and China. One of Georg Gidal's most impressive reportages was his winter ascent of the Great St. Bernard Pass and the rescue of an injured person by St. Bernard dogs during a snowstorm.

Man's reportage picture of Mussolini in his study was published in number nine of the *MIP*, and again as a full-page photo in number eleven.

Willi Ruge photographed himself during a parachute jump. In the same issue in which it appeared, the *Berliner* began publishing some excellent sports photos by Lothar Rübelt. These were no longer single pictures of an event, but complete reportages on double-page spreads.

The famous pilot Udet took a Leica with him on his travels in Africa and photographed lions leaping at his low-flying aircraft.

Weber's sociological reportage on the "Village Without Work" was followed by reports on poverty-stricken villages, on a women's prison, on gamblers secretly photographed in the casino, a moving reportage on mental patients in a theater performance, and pictures taken in a deaf-and-dumb school.

The reportage with the greatest impact even today is that which Bosshard made of a Zeppelin flight to the Arctic regions. During this journey the Zeppelin met the Russian icebreaker *Malygin*. As a boat from the *Malygin* approached the Zeppelin (which had landed on the ice), Bosshard recognized the North Pole explorer Umberto Nobile in the background. (Amundsen perished in 1928 while searching for Nobile, while Nobile returned home safe and sound, subsequently to become an adviser to the Russian airplane industry.) Lincoln Ellsworth was in the Zeppelin at the time. "It was for me," wrote Bosshard, "the most moving moment of the journey as I recognized Nobile with a pained smile on his face in a corner on the deck of the *Malygin*." Bosshard photographed this moment; another picture shows Nobile holding out his hand in response to Ellsworth's greeting.

Whether his pictures show an animated conversation between the great and diametrically opposed scientists, Planck and Einstein, during a reception; a dramatic reunion between Nobile and Ellsworth; the first report on the "interior life" of Oxford University; or life in a women's prison—Bosshard never fails to provide vivid first-hand experiences of the life of the time.

Man's reportages, too, now were being published in the *Berliner*. His first reportage dealt with life in a night shelter. In December 1930, the *BIZ* published the first reportage by a photographer who had just begun to create complete series of pictures as well as single images. This was Alfred Eisenstaedt's sensitive "Ballet School."

The *MIP* continued to publish large-scale photoreportages every week: nightlife in London (Weber); a Swiss college for tubercular patients (Man); a controversial three-page report of a French gambling casino (E. P. Hahn); Man's famous photointerview with Mussolini; unforgettable pictures of Charlie Chaplin at a children's dance in Berlin (Hübschmann); a theater performance by mental patients (Weber); "Waiting-room for Heaven"—the Fuggerei in Augsburg (Tim Gidal); the Saint Maurice monastery school (Georg Gidal); voluntary labor service (Georg and Tim Gidal); deaf-and-dumb school (Weber); abandoned coal mines—unemployment in the Rhineland (Man); the death of the pedestrian (Man).

Between 1929 and 1931, the photoreportage expanded to cover all areas of life. The world in front of the lens had become its natural environment. The photoreportage, now on a level with the written report, was accorded recognition as an expansion and enrichment of journalism. During this time, fine ethnological reportages were published on the Near East, Africa, and Yemen by J. von Heimburg, Harald Lechenperg, H. A. Bernatzik, and Hans Helfritz.

New magazines modeled on the *Berliner* and the *Münchner* appeared in other countries, and a number of existing journals went over to the new form of photojournalism. Among them were *Vu* in Paris under its editor-in-chief Lucien Vogel. Founded in 1928, it soon became the most "modern" and successful magazine in France. The *Zürcher* was the leading publication in Switzerland. The *Leipziger Illustrirte*, the *Schweizer Illustrierte*, and *L'Illustration*, as well as the English and American magazines remained conservative and thus outdated for some time to come. The themes of these publications remained on the level of "Handmade Pillow Lace," "The Wonderful World of Flowers," "The Finest Pictures from the Royal Academy," "The Life of the Eskimos," and "The Opening of the Spring Session of the Swiss Federal Parliament in Berne," (an empty parliament building and empty rooms). The picture story in reportage style made slow progress in these magazines.

With the exception of the party magazines, *AIZ* (Communist) and the *Illustrierte Beobachter* (Nazi), German magazines were and remained independent in editorial content. The editors-in-chief, nearly all liberal-minded, were not influenced by the political views of their publishers. Their aim was to set forth basic aspects of the life of the time, honest statements presented in an interesting manner, even if this meant showing the negative sides of the social structure. Thus a retrospective view of the German illustrated magazines of 1932 provides a true reflection of an era full of contradictions and uncertainty.

The themes dealt with in 1932 bore little resemblance to those of the preceding years. Three years earlier, Salomon reported on the traditional Munich Carnival in the *MIP*; in 1930, it was Man; in 1931, Wolfgang Weber and Stwolinsky, and in 1932, Lorant gave me the commission. My pictures showed Klaus and Erika Mann, the great actress Therese Giehse, the "Zeus of Schwabing" Karl Wolfskehl, and disciples of Stefan George. It was the last time that "Schwabylon" came together during Carnival in the legendary Pension Fürmann, where Rilke and the "Schwabing Aphrodite," Countess Reventlow, had lived, and where the "wahnmochinger" Dionysiac festivities of the George circle were celebrated, with George and Wolfskehl and beautiful women and boys. The two-faced Ludwig Klages also participated as did the pseudo-philosopher Alfred Schuler. Among Schuler's "blood-and-soil"-maddened disciples, Adolf Hitler could be found. There was dancing on a powder barrel and kissing on the pirate's plank, but we became aware of this only in retrospect.

The *Münchner* published a photoreportage entitled "Stock Exchange Closed: Wall Street 1932." The unemployed sold apples on the street without accusing any specific ethnic group. Side by side with a photo retrospective of the terrible inflation period and the Spartacus struggles, there was a reportage entitled "A Quiet Valley—the City Dweller's Dream." Neudin uncovered for us the building up of a new and ill-concealed secret army, "With Wooden Guns and Cardboard Tanks," and England's darker side was revealed in Eisenstaedt's "London's Slums." Flash photographs of nocturnal cavalry exercises were admired for their camera skill and daring.

The *Berliner* presented "Our Tanks" (wooden models), a reportage on a youth hostel, "A Roof for the Night," and another report on voluntary labor service. No one noticed the ominous lightning on the political horizon.

Almost all the feature films of these years were far removed from the realism of the new photoreportage. Artificial and ambitious, they imitated the expressionistic "Caligarism" which had animated German cinema in the twenties. There were exceptions: the Chaplin films, Dreyer's *Joan of Arc*, von Sternberg's *The Last Command* with Emil Jannings, and *The Blue Angel* with Marlene Dietrich and Jannings. Bergner's movies and the great Russian films also were fresh. Two thirds of all motion pictures produced in 1930 were still silent—not necessarily a disadvantage for most of them, which were mediocre and mawkish. There were a few that were different, related as they were to the style of the new photoreportage: Robert O'Flaherty's documentary *Nanook of the North*, which was filmed in 1922 and ran for a long period, and Calvalcanti's *Rien que les Heures* (1926), which traced the life of an individual over twenty-four hours. Most outstanding, however, was Moriz Seeler's *People on Sunday* (1929), a film showing a Sunday in the lives of four white-collar workers. The main characters were a shop assistant, a traveling salesman, a movie extra, and a chauffeur, all of them amateurs. Pudovkin's *Mother* and Nicolai Ekk's *The Path into Life* were also noteworthy.

Apart from the *Berliner* and the *Münchner*, the *Kölnische* (under the editorship of Erwin Berghaus and Paul Feinhals, who died in 1932 also published many photoreportages. The *AIZ* was chiefly devoted to social criticism and Communist propaganda, and among its contributors and advisers were George Grosz and John Heartfield, whose powerful and unequaled photomontages highlighted the political difficulties and economic distress of the working classes.

The *AIZ* presented reportages such as "Father Goes Out Begging," "Unemployed," "Pilgrimage for Bread," and "How the Rich Live." A series, reprinted from a Russian magazine, entitled "Twenty-four Hours in the Life of a Working-Class Family in Moscow," was particularly informative, and the idea was seized upon by others and adapted to German conditions. The *AIZ* frequently offered fresh ideas and experimented with new forms of presentation, at times devising striking contrasts for the cover page. For the most part, however, the texts were manipulated politically. Georg Gidal's text to his reportage on the seasonal hops-pickers in Lower Bavaria was replaced by a text filled with party clichés: "The overseers and helpers of the hops-barons select the strongest men for their hops-fields and the prettiest girls for their beds." The *Kölnische Illustrierte* published the same pictures a few weeks later with Gidal's original text. Shortly afterward, the *AIZ* published my reportage "Hamburg by Night," and here, too, genuine social grievances were made less credible or falsified through political slogans in captions by the editors. From then on, we stopped working for the *AIZ*. Like all the other photoreporters mentioned, we had forbidden our agencies to submit our pictures to the Nazi *Illustrierte Beobachter* from the very beginning. This magazine manipulated the texts and captions in much the same way as the *AIZ*. The objectivity of the photograph causes the viewer to be less critical, allowing him to be greatly influenced by a manipulating caption. The high level of the documentary photoreportage and the progressive style of presentation in the *AIZ* was almost always accompanied by over-simplified slogans. The style of the *Illustrierte Beobachter*, in contrast, was amateurish, the text and captions inflammatory. These two magazines proved that the way a caption is written can either explain and elucidate the picture or falsify its statement.

When we look back over the German illustrated magazines from 1929 to 1933, we observe that except for Salomon, each of the photoreporters mentioned was outstanding in a specific area although they reported on a wide variety of subjects. To paraphrase Ibsen, the photoreportage can be called the reproduction of nature seen through the eyes of a specific temperament. An examination of the individual reporter's main interests yields the following result:

Walter Bosshard	The adventure of human life. Appeal to human justice.
Georg Gidal	Mankind in professional life and leisure time. The child's world.
Tim Gidal	Gestures and expressions. Man in the community.
Kurt Hübschmann	Sympathy and joy of life.
Felix H. Man	Human society in its interesting moments.
Martin Munkacsi	Beauty in all its forms. The single picture in the reportage.

Neudin	The adventure of human life. Social conditions and institutions.
Erich Salomon	The atmosphere of political discussions. Psychological photos of great personalities in the fields of science, politics, and art.
Umbo	The photographic experience.
Wolfgang Weber	Social criticism. Sensation in human life and sensation in the reportage.

This group made up the core of the photoreporters of the time. There were two more: André Kertesz, who produced only three or four reportage series during these years; and Alfred Eisenstaedt, who first appeared on the reportage scene at the end of 1931.

André Kertesz	The poetic moment in human life.
Alfred Eisenstaedt	The intuitive perception of the moment with regard to publication.

The most hard-working reporters were probably Georg Gidal, Man, Neudin, Salomon, and Wolfgang Weber, each producing about twenty-five reportages a year. And "produced" almost always meant "published." Most of the photoreportages were republished in slightly altered form by other magazines following initial publication.

There were not many photojournalists who created reportages according to their own ideas and who delivered text and pictures both. The few who rose above the anonymous mass of photographers were recognized by their bylines signed to their contributions. They were much in demand and were paid accordingly. Ten to twenty marks were paid for a single picture. But for first publication of a series of five to fifteen pictures, photoreporters received anything from two hundred to two thousand marks. "The independent photoreporter," wrote one editor-in-chief, "represents an entirely new type of journalist who must be regarded as a kind of special correspondent. He leaves nothing to chance when pursuing the subject of his interest, and he seeks to present it in the best and most suitable form by means of intensive preparatory work. He cannot begin without the basic idea, by which he must be virtually obsessed. Thus the intellectual and artistic achievement of a genuine photoreportage cannot be overestimated."

The common denominator shared by the great photoreporters was the combination of (1) a talent for observation and the ability to experience and participate intensely, and (2) sensitivity, empathy, and intuition for capturing the essential quality of the whole in the single picture. The religious philosopher Martin Buber wrote in his book on education: "Every living situation has a new face, like a newborn child, despite all similarity to previous situations, something which has never before existed and which will never be repeated... it requires presence, responsibility, and you yourself."

Munkacsi and Umbo both possessed sure feeling for form in the composition of their pictures. Whether this aesthetic element was concentrated on the purely formal aspect and strengthened the documentary content of the reportage, or had a weakening influence by virtue of the greater subjectivity which it implied, is not a theme for discussion here.

As regards myself, I photographed what interested me, regardless of whether I had been commissioned to do so or not. I was moved by the meeting of the vagabonds—there were so many men, old and young, from all walks of life: vagrants, handworkers, artists, academic drop-outs, eternal wanderers. Their heroes were often literary figures as described by Knut Hamsun and Hermann Hesse; their break with society was in no case accidental. The conversation touched on Siddharta, the pilgrim Kamanita, human life, and freedom. They were related to the hippies of our day, but there was one essential difference: the achievement of a certain age did not automatically imply a spiritual and intellectual paralysis. It was not age which counted, rather a basic dynamism. The cultural pessimism of the postwar years was clearly manifested in this group although —or perhaps because—it was lived out in the form of negation. This became clear in discussions with an ex-teacher, for example, who had given up his position (which carried a pension) in order, as he put it, to retain his inner freedom.

"This applies only to me!" he emphasized. "Every individual must find his own way in life." And he added thoughtfully: "Do you know what I taught my pupils? *'Dulc' ét decórum' st pró patriá morí'*—It is sweet and honorable to die for the Fatherland.... And if they recited it with the wrong accent, they were punished. Have you any idea for whom or what my pupils sweetly and honorably died in the last war before they were able to fulfill themselves? I am always happy to hear the economic situation is sound. When it isn't, there is the danger of a dictator emerging like in Italy. After all, we no longer have Kaiser Wilhelm. And then it will be sweet and honorable once more. Look over there, there's a good guitarist. Let's go and listen..."

It seems to me that I always encountered the same basic themes in my reportages: how does man live, how does he fit into his society, and what is the life of this society. I also tried to report on subjects of current political interest.

At the beginning of 1930 I traveled to Palestine to make a number of reportages on the tension between Jews and Arabs. These reportages appeared in the *MIP*, the *Woche*, the *Kölnische*, and many other publications. Political reportages of this kind had become an essential part of photojournalism. It was in this year that Bosshard's outstanding reports from India were published.

Every photoreporter of the time experimented in the quest for new themes and techniques, but real originality was comparatively rare. We were all passionate practitioners in a new territory, and we had to do our best with the new aspects and occasions that confronted us. In this sense, every photoreporter in these three years was the "first" although, whether or not we were aware of it, our achievements were not always as new as they might have seemed.

In general, we disdained the use of flash. The new cameras could take interior pictures in available light and thus avoid disturbing the atmosphere of the occasion. But as I wandered through the dark, narrow streets of Hamburg at night, it became clear that a reportage without flash would not be possible. A picture taken with an Ermanox on a tripod in the unrelieved darkness could produce no results even with exposures of ten seconds, and so I bought a flash. Neudin helped me by igniting the charge of approximately ten grams when I gave the word, and we then vanished through back streets we had inspected by day. Furtive visitors to brothels would hardly have appreciated the presence of a prowling photographer. After this first experience, however, I never used an open flash again, though later I sometimes made use of a closed one. This enabled me to capture a scene's natural air, which the frontal flash upset. However, we cannot overcome the disadvantage of an ordinary flash in complete darkness disturbing the documentary value of the picture—just as much today as in the photos of Riis and Hine.

The great comedian Karl Valentin was later to teach me a method of achieving "natural" flash pictures. I was preparing to photograph him at his workbench when he said, "Oh dear, any moment now it'll start to stink!" I asked, "What do you mean?" "Where's your flash, then?" he replied, "I can hardly see what I'm doing!" I told him, "I don't need a flash, the light over your head is sufficient if I expose at a fifth of a second, and the result will be a natural picture." "And a natural blur!" was his retort. "Don't be stubborn. We can put in a stronger light bulb, and then you can make a reasonable exposure to achieve the same result. But personally I would prefer flash. You're not a proper photographer without it!"

He inserted a brighter bulb, and I took the picture with a fortieth instead of a fifth of a second. However, his remarks made me think. When the closed flash became available, I used it often for pictures of rapid movement indoors. The confusion of Carnival time was an example of this. I did not flash frontally, however, but asked a friend to ignite the flash from a point next to a ceiling lamp for the exposure. The friend always came dressed as a chimney-sweep, installed his ladder under a lamp, and waited for my signal.

Since about 1950, photoreporters have used the "bounced flash" method to reproduce the effect of natural interior lighting. It is done by pointing the electronic flash toward the ceiling from where it is reflected as a much stronger ceiling light. Essentially, this is a development of Karl Valentin's idea.

V. Editing, Layout, Captions

Until the emergence of modern photojournalism, illustrated papers sought to present themes which "entertained and informed" the reader. The documentary photo emphasized the informational function.

The new photojournalism enlarged this basic function by challenging the reader to participate. The permanence of this desired reaction, however, was largely determined by the graphic presentation, in other words, by the layout of the material, and the personality of the editor-in-chief. It was his task to present to best advantage the content and mood of a humanly felt photoreportage, taking into consideration the text and the captions. The new type of editor-in-chief recognized the essential character and significance of this style of reportage which was charged with human emotion and made a strong human statement. This was true whether the reportage dealt with serious problems or light-hearted subjects. He was the director, so to speak, of the new photojournalism, the photoreportage, the photostory, and the photoessay. It was possible now to present not only the event itself, but also the reactions of participants and spectators by their gestures and facial expressions. Such photos enabled the reader to identify with the statement of the reportage. Thus there arose a lively interaction between the photoreporter and the reader.

As a result, the photoreportage acquired an importance equal to that of the written word as a contemporary journalistic medium at the beginning of visual mass communications. The size of the picture was no longer determined by the number of words. Quite the contrary: the photoreport, dynamic and complete in itself, dictated the length of the text.

The graphic concept, concerned with balance and proportion, determined both the inner tension of the single image and the relationship of the pictures to each other.

A dynamic and harmonious unity was created thereby, formed largely by the artistic concept of the editor-in-chief.

In the early years of photojournalism, text and captions were left all too often to journalists "borrowed" for this purpose from daily newspapers owned by the same publisher who owned the magazine. The dubious and uncertain connections of such writers to the new medium frequently resulted in condescending, inadequate, and so-called impressionistic captions. Quotations by Schiller, Goethe, and other classic writers were used to bridge any gap, as for example in the caption to the main picture in Man's "Swimming Pool in Lunapark."

Researched texts and objective captions were traditional and essential elements in British journalism, which influenced the European magazines. The great variety possible is revealed by the following list of captions that could all be written for a picture of celebrations of discharged Swiss soldiers at the end of their two-week reservist service. The soldiers are shown marching onto Münsterplatz in Basel.

1. *(objective):*
   March of local militia soldiers before their discharge on Münsterplatz.
2. *(explanatory):*
   It is a well-known fact that Switzerland possesses a militia whose members must attend a fortnight's military training course each year, following an initial course of two months. Our picture shows...
3. *(patriotic, political accent):*
   Once again, our proud soldiers return from a period of military training—a particularly valuable public service when we consider the closeness of the national borders...
4. *(local information):*
   Anyone present at the Münsterplatz this morning was confronted by a lively spectacle. Under a radiant blue sky, accompanied by traditional marches played by a military band, our proud soldiers returned...
5. *(critical, negative):*
   Our Swiss bourgeoisie is not prepared to do without its coveted militarism...
6. *(aesthetic, atmospheric):*
   A view of the marching troops from the tower of the Basel Cathedral. A highly artistic picture which shows both the beauty of the Münsterplatz and the equally impressive perfection of the soldiers in formation.
7. *(technical):*
   A picture taken with wide-angle lens from the tower of Basel Cathedral. This was the only way possible to capture both the interesting perspective of the square and a wide but partial view of the city.
8. *(topical report):*
   A march of the militia men onto the Münsterplatz took place at this year's celebrations. During the speech by Colonel X., Lance-Corporal Y's horse bolted, and it was only the quick thinking of a soldier named Max Buser, of Peterskirchplatz 113 and a precision-tool maker by profession, which prevented the...
9. *(shortest form, patriotic):*
   "Hail Helvetia—these are your sons!"

We see by these examples that there is almost always a subjective element pointing in a particular direction. In general, however, the objective, explanatory caption is only slowly becoming the accepted form in the illustrated magazines.

VI. Nineteen-Thirty-Three

In January 1933, Adolf Hitler was named chancellor of the German Reich by President Hindenburg. In February, the Reichstag was burned to the ground. The new Chancellor banned the Communist Party, and the Communist delegates were deprived of their seats in the Reichstag, to the advantage of a right-wing coalition. The right-wing parties, ready to compromise, supported Hitler's seizure of power in March.

The illustrated magazines published reports of these events, but no one knew what might follow. The discussions were concerned chiefly with whether the situation would last eight weeks or eight months.

In February, *MIP* brought out its traditional Carnival issue. *BIZ* and *MIP* published reports in March and April of more than three or six pages on "Germany's Greatest Hour" and "Celebrations in Potsdam." On February 19, *AIZ* published a cover picture entitled "For Work, Bread, and Freedom" and a photoreport "Six Days and Twelve More Killings by Hitler's Murderers." This was the last issue of *AIZ* to appear in Germany. Its offices were broken into, and the building was burned down on Hitler's orders. Most of the editors were forced to flee and escaped to Prague.

Number eleven of the *MIP* still carried the name of Stefan Lorant as editor-in-chief. But when number twelve appeared he was already in prison, having been arrested on March 14. The *BIZ* number twelve shows the name of Friedrich Trefz as "representing" Kurt Korff. Korff had fled to the United States, but the *BIZ* continued nonetheless to list him as editor until number thirteen. In number fourteen, he was replaced by Carl Schnebel.

One of the many Nazi "achievements" of these months was the collapse of the new photojournalism. Good reportages by Wolfgang Weber continued to appear, however, as did a number of single pictures and reportages by Munkacsi and Eisenstaedt who remained in Germany until 1935. Work by Lechenperg, Hubmann, the Schwabik brothers, and Werner Cohnitz was appearing more frequently. But the greater part of their pictures consisted of propagandistic material. The illustrated magazines had lost their independence.

In one of the best-known propaganda pictures of the time, the new Führer can be seen plodding up a mountain through a line of swastika bearers. He is carrying his hat as if he had raised it to himself, and he regards his subjects with a certain element of misgiving. The caption runs: "Hundreds of thousands line the path from the foot of the mountain to the platform at the summit." A few years later, a mountain of 25 million bodies was to lie beneath the trampling feet of the Führer—among them many of those who had lined his path.

Korff and Szafranski went to the United States, followed by Birnbach and, later on, Alfred Eisenstaedt and the head of his agency, Daniel, as well as Munkacsi and Mayer, the owner of the photoagency Mauritius. Salomon fled to Holland where the Germans later discovered and killed him.

A reporter new on the scene, Robert Capa, went to Paris, as did Goro. Hübschmann and Man went to England, followed by Simon Gutmann. I went to Switzerland and completed my studies in Basel. At one blow, most of the established photoreporters and the most important agencies stopped work. Birnbach, Daniel, and Mayer established photoagencies in New York. Korff and Szafranski were later involved in setting up *Life* magazine. In 1936, Eisenstaedt became one of the first photoreporters of this new periodical. Munkacsi became one of the most sought-after photographers in New York.

Stefan Lorant was released from prison in 1933 after intervention by the Hungarian government. He went to Budapest where he was made editor-in-chief of the photogravure Sunday supplement to the paper *Pesti Naplo*—a magazine twice as large in size as the German magazines. Thus Lorant was able to create a large-format magazine according to his own ideas. In 1934, he moved to London, where he became editor of the *Weekly Illustrated*, and in 1938, he was appointed editor-in-chief of the newly founded *Picture Post*. Hübschmann, Man, and Gidal were his chief collaborators on this magazine.

Why did these men, who were so integrally bound up with the origin and success of German photojournalism, feel obliged to leave Germany? Man was not Jewish, nor was Munkacsi, most likely. The rest were. Hübschmann was half Jewish. It is an interesting phenomenon that so many Jews possessed this specific talent for photojournalism, similar to that of the many Jewish film directors (Lang, Wilder, Capa, Korda, Lubitsch, von Sternberg, Vertov, Eisenstein, and others). Perhaps it was a reaction to the centuries-old restraints in this field. According to a now controversial Biblical command, Jews were forbidden to create images of human beings. When this restriction was lifted during the intellectual liberation which followed their assimilation, the creative forces hitherto suppressed were set free with an explosive impact.

1933 saw the decline of photojournalism in Germany. In that year, a second generation of photoreporters in other countries emerged and joined the pioneers. Together they determined the face of photoreportage in France (Capa, Chim, Cartier-Bresson), in Switzerland (Werner Bischof and Gotthard Schuh), in the United States (Dorothea Lange, Walter Crane, Margaret Bourke-White, Arthur Rothstein, Carl Mydans). This second generation was similar to the first in its inner relationship to the photoreportage and in the manner of its visual composition.

The photoreporter has survived all aesthetic and technical trends and fashions. He pays little or no attention to them since he does not use the drawbacks, peculiarities, and possibilities of technology in photography in the interests of individual expression or new effects. Rather he accepts them as existing necessities. Only thus is it possible to explain the timeless persistence of the photoreporter from Fenton until today. The new photojournalism, which originated in Germany and which is served by the written word, has become a visual document of social history. With the help of visual media it has inaugurated a new era of mass communications. Here lies its historical importance, past and present.

Captions to the illustrations will be found on pages 94 and 95.

Walter Bosshard

18. Mai 1930
7. Jahrgang / Nr. 20

Münchner Illustri[…] Presse

Erscheint wöchentlich
Preis: 20 Pfennig

Knorr & Hirth, München

Der Mann, der das britische Weltreich herausgefordert hat:

Mahatma Gandhi liest

(Diese Aufnahme und die im Innern des Blattes veröffentlichten stammen von unserem Mitarbeiter Walter Boßhard, dem einzigen in Gandhis Lager zugelassenen Europäer)

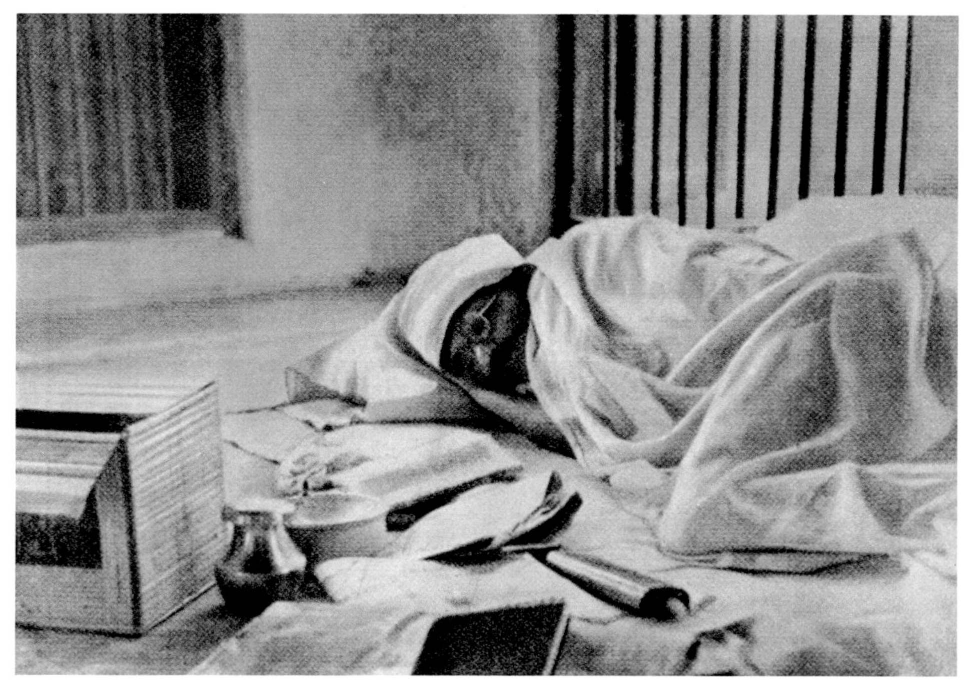

Blick vom Zeppelin auf den „Malygin" am verabredeten Treffpunkt, der Hooker-Bucht.

Auf der Fahrt vom „Malygin" zum „Zeppelin".
Aufnahmen: Boßhard.

Wie die russischen Besucher vom Boot aus den Zeppelin sahen:
Luftschiff und Eisbrecher lagen wegen der Funkengefahr aus dem Schornstein des „Malygin" mehrere hundert Meter voneinander entfernt.

Felix H. Man

25. August 1929
Nummer 34
38. Jahrgang

Berliner

Illustrirte Zeitung

Verlag Ullstein Berlin SW 68

Preis des Heftes 20 Pfennig

Abendgespräch im Haag.

Reichsaußenminister Dr. Stresemann, der Führer der deutschen Delegation auf der Haager Konferenz, beim deutschen Gesandten Grafen Zech.

ZWISCHEN MITTERNAC
UND MORGENGRAU

am Kurfürstendamm

Ein Streifzug mit der Kamera durch die westliche Hauptstraße von Berlin

Dieser viel geliebte, viel verdammte, viel umdichtete, viel verleumdete, viel besungene, viel mißverstandene, viel gemalte Damm ist ja gar kein Damm; jedenfalls kein gewöhnlicher, kein einfacher Damm, schon weil er zwei Dämme hat, einen fürs Hin und den anderen fürs Zurück, wobei der linke Damm nicht weiß, was der rechte tut. Der ganze Asphaltstreifen, der sich da protzig, geschäftig, temperamentvoll, müßig durch Berlins wildesten Westen zieht, reagiert wie eine penible Frauenseele auf jede Stunde, Temperatur, Konjunktur, Sonne, Wolke, Börse, Messe, Mode, Politik, Szene, Welle und Zeit. Doch nie hat ihn je einer müde gesehen. Im Gegenteil: hier findet ob Mitternacht das einzig garantiert echte Weltstadt-Nachtleben statt, allerdings nur zwischen Kirche und Uhlandstraße mit Hauptstützungspunkt an der drei Baedeker-Sterne würdigen Ecke Joachimsthaler.

Die Theater sind aus
Auto folgt auf Auto

Kaum verlöschen die Lichtmassen müder Konditoreien Schlag zwölf, prinseln die ersten Nachtschwärmer zage an, besetzen zunächst die wichtigsten Ausguck-Nischen, stehen herum und gaffen, weil's hier immerzu was zu bestaunen gibt. Endlose Reihen heimwärts pilgernder Bürger. Die paar Bänke sind noch von Schaulustigen ausverkauft. Die Restaurants und Kabaretts schütten ihre Häuser aus. Aufläufe mit grimmigen Boxereien entstehen an den Haltestellen vor jeder der vermeintlich letzten Bahnen und Bussen. Kragenfreie Kolonnen Straßenarbeiter marschieren auf, stellen Warnlampen hin, buddeln, hämmern, ziehen tagslaut zählend gleichmäßig an

Die dritte Schicht!
Straßenarbeit vor der Gedächtniskirche

Nach Mitternacht vor dem Kaffee

. . . und der Grüne wacht!

einem Kabel, schieben Schienen. Ein über
Kommando-Auto trompetet an den erschre
Bürgersteigen vorüber. So manches Zu
häuslerherz schlägt ruhiger, wenn der bü
Wagen in der Ferne verschwindet. Ein G
mann, wie aus vergangenen Jahrzehnten, d
mit seiner langen Stange die große Pr
beleuchtung aus, läßt in jedem Gasballon
zwei Funzeln surren. Droschken schleichen
auf Kundenfang vorüber. Generalsunifo
locken vor jeder Bar zum Eintritt. Zweis
gondeln vorüber. Mit glücklichen Pärchen,
auch nur mit einem allein am Steuer, der f
süchtig nach einer Begleiterin auslugt.
meisten Restaurants schließen. Es wird geb
düsterer. Musiker und Kellner eilen sachlic
die nächsten Haltestellen.

Voller wird es auf den Bürgersteigen.
Frauen und Männern aller Alter, Breiten
Klassen. Die schlendern, weil sie nicht sch
können oder nicht wollen, allein oder auc
zweien und dreien immer wie auf dem B
mel auf und ab. Nachtwächter, wie Adm
uniformiert, klimpern mit ihren Schlüsseln
Hunden vorüber. Schutzpolizei tendelt

„Der Penner"
Er schläft nur, bis der nächste Schupo kommt

Das Nachtlokal leert sich
Man wartet auf die Wagen

Das andere Gesicht
des Kurfürstendammes

Wurst-Maxe schlägt sich der
von der Michels-Ecke mit dem
-Händler aus der Tauentzien
eines Mädels. Zwei Ehepaare
en mit Rucksack und je drei
nden Göhren an irgend einen
Frühzug. Die letzten Punkte
Bars erlöschen. Ein vergesse-
tehumlegekragen läßt sich vom
ind übern Asphalt rutschen.
agen und Gemüsekarren, mit
Menschen bepackt, ruckeln in

die Halle. Eine Lokomotive pfeift vom nahen Zoo. Die Kirchenuhr bummert schon fünfe. Die ersten leeren Straßenbahnen fauchen aus ihren Höfen. Die Gaslampen pfeifen, alle wie auf einen Wink, aus. Schupos marschieren zu Dreien. Ein Schaufenster klirrt. Zeitungsautos tuten. Hinter der Tauentzien graut der Morgen.

Schlechter Geschäftsgang!
Die Zeitungsfrau ist eingeschlafen

Aufnahmen: Dephot Man

Viel Begeisterung, viel Kraftverbrauch ...
Eine Aufruhrszene wird geprobt

Ein geborener Komiker?
Er fühlt sich als kommenden Chaplin, Harald Lloyd oder Buster Keaton

Alle hoffen auf die große Filmzukunft
Schülerinnen aus einer Berliner Filmschule

Filmstar für M. 1.50

Vor den Ruhm haben die Götter die Zahlung von RM. 1.50 gesetzt

Aufnahmen aus einer Berliner Filmschule von Man (Dephot)

Eine merkwürdige Gesellschaft kommt da am Abend zusammen: junge Leute, die den Weg zum Ruhm suchen, die Verwirklichung des großen Hollywood-Traumes. Sie kommen zusammen, weil sie sich in ihrem Beruf unbefriedigt, häufig auch unglücklich fühlen, sie wollen etwas Höheres erreichen, Ruhm und Reichtum, kurz: sie wollen Filmstar werden. Im westlichsten Westen Berlins sammelt sich diese Träumergesellschaft; schon das ist eine Traum-Verwirklichung, sie sind ja Kinder des weiten Ostens und des Nordens, doch Ruhm und Reichtum hausen im Westen, also kommen sie, müde nach der Tagesarbeit, zahlen ihr Lehrgeld und betreten hier den Weg, der unmittelbar nach Hollywood, jedoch zumindest nach Neubabelsberg führen sollte.

Das eine muß man ihnen lassen: Begeisterung haben

(Fortsetzung auf Seite 424)

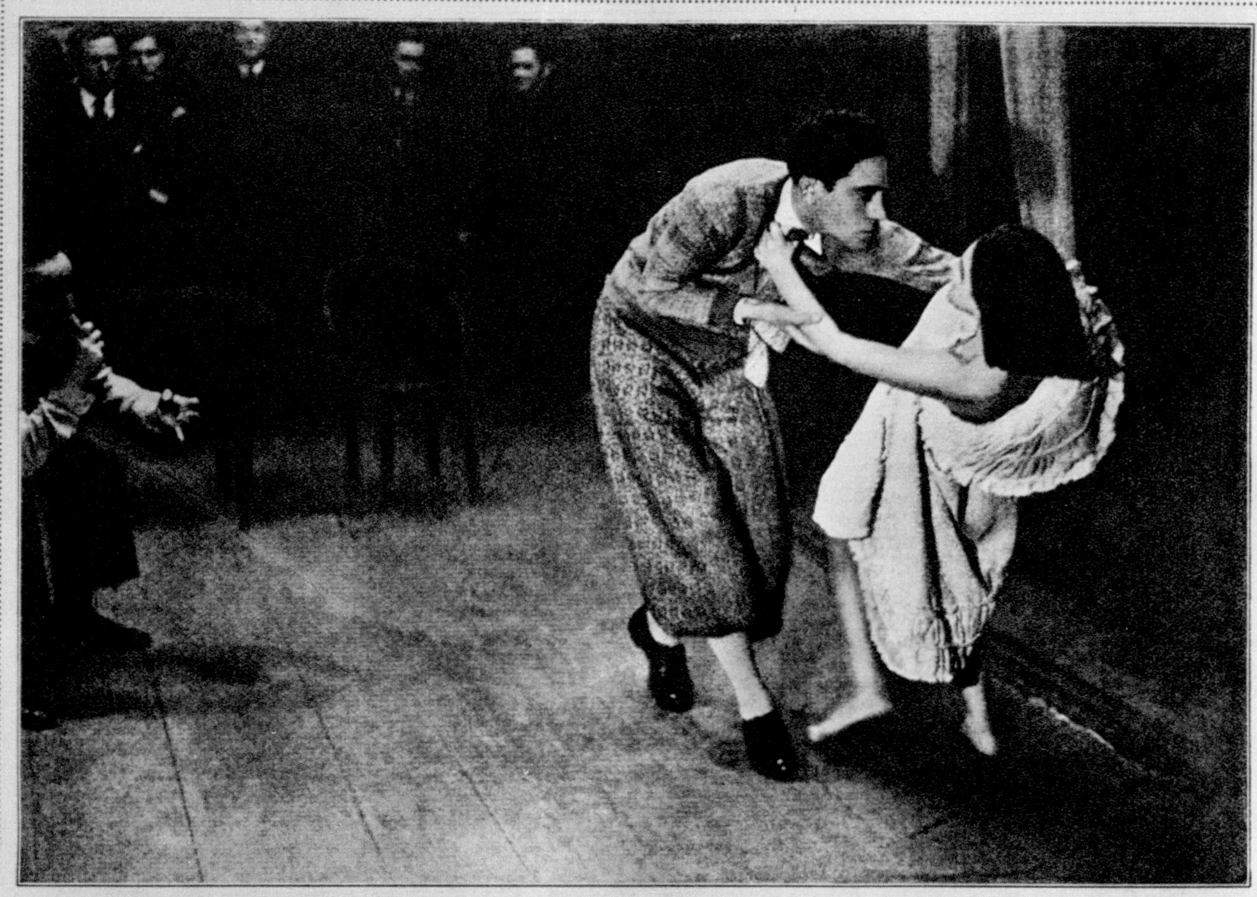

Der wilde Verführer

Das Wichtigste an diesem Bild ist der Regisseur der Filmschule (links). Er gibt mit der Pfeife sofort das Signal wenn das Bild sich nicht mehr für die Zensur eignet

Mord und Totschlag

Der Lehrer erklärt, wie man vor der Kamera spielt:

Er zeigt nämlich gerade, wie ein richtiger Straßenhändler (mit Hosenträgern) im Film auftritt und die dicke Dame nimmt sich ein Beispiel daran

Mutter, dein Kind geriet auf Abwege!

Phot. Man (Dephot)

(Diese Szene einer Mutter, der ein Brief verriet, was die Tochter ihr nun nicht länger verheimlichen kann, greift jedem Fühlenden ans Herz).

Dr. Erich Salomon

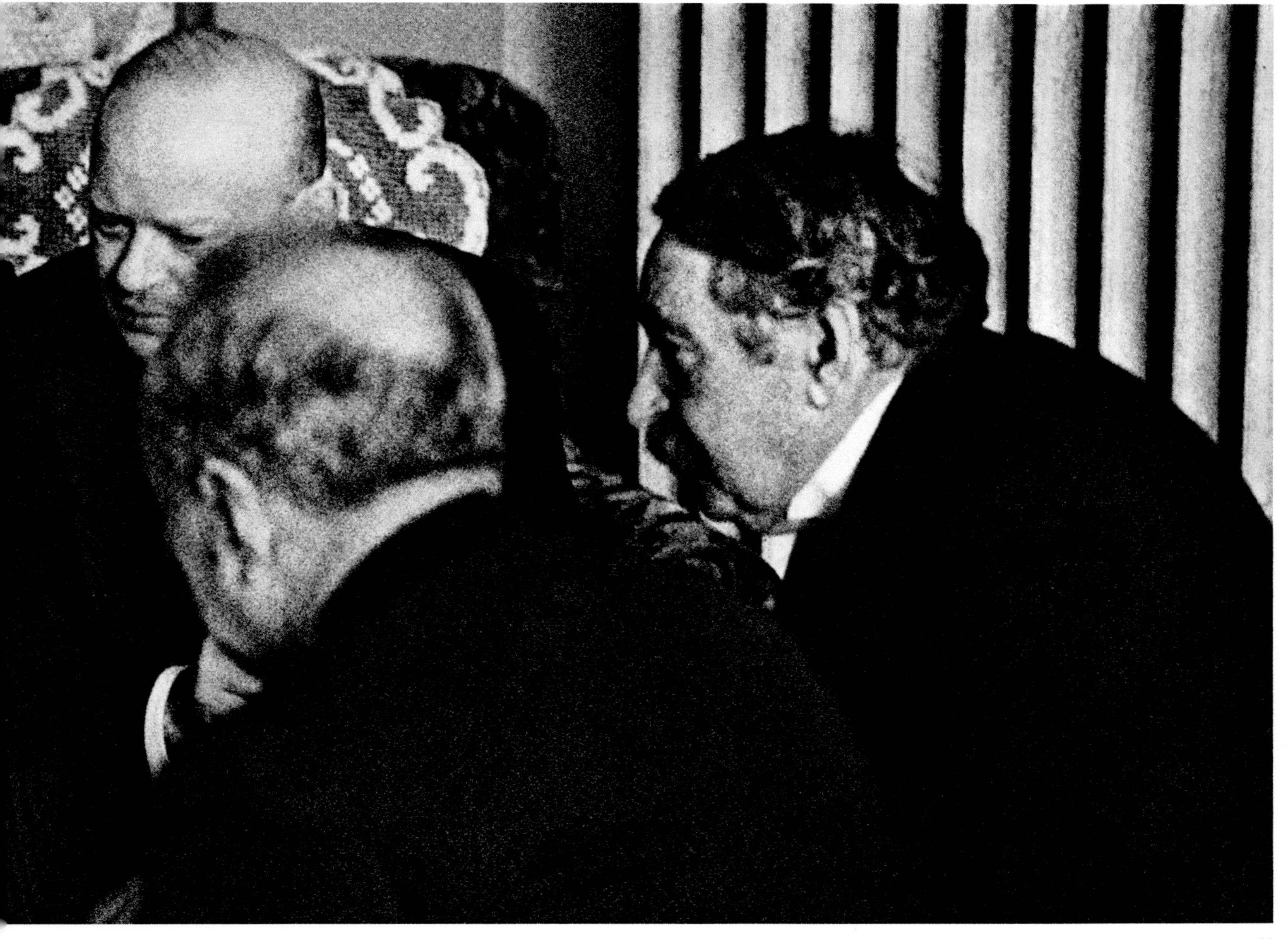

Wolfgang Weber

ummer 36. 6. September 1931. 40. Jahrgang. Preis 20 Pfennig

Berliner Illustrirte Zeitung

Verlag Ullstein Berlin SW 68

„Wir wollen kein Krisengeld, keine Fürsorge ... nur irgendeine Arbeit, Straßenbau, Land roden ... irgend etwas!"
Ein erschütterndes Bild deutscher Not, das unser Fotograf unbemerkt im Bürgermeisteramt des fränkischen Dörfchens Wallenfels aufnahm.
Hierzu der Artikel „Das Dorf ohne Arbeit" auf den nächsten Seiten. Fot. Wolfgang Weber.

P.D.R. HUDSon
WH-128

Martin Munkacsi

Willi Ruge

Alfred Eisenstaedt

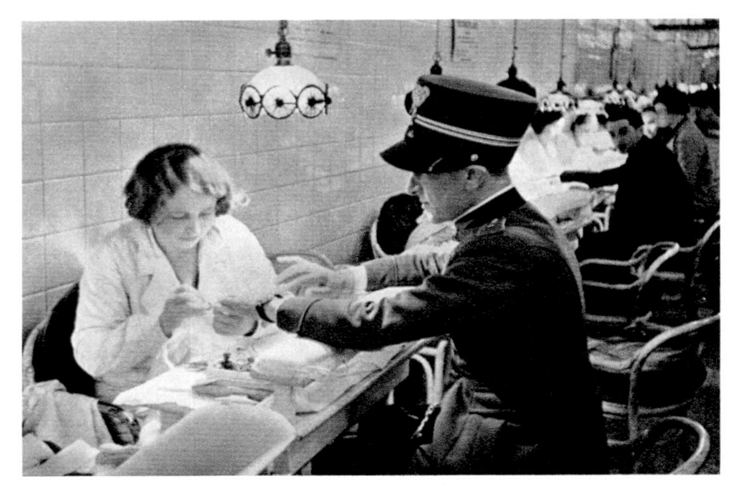

Dr. Tim N. Gidal

André Kertész

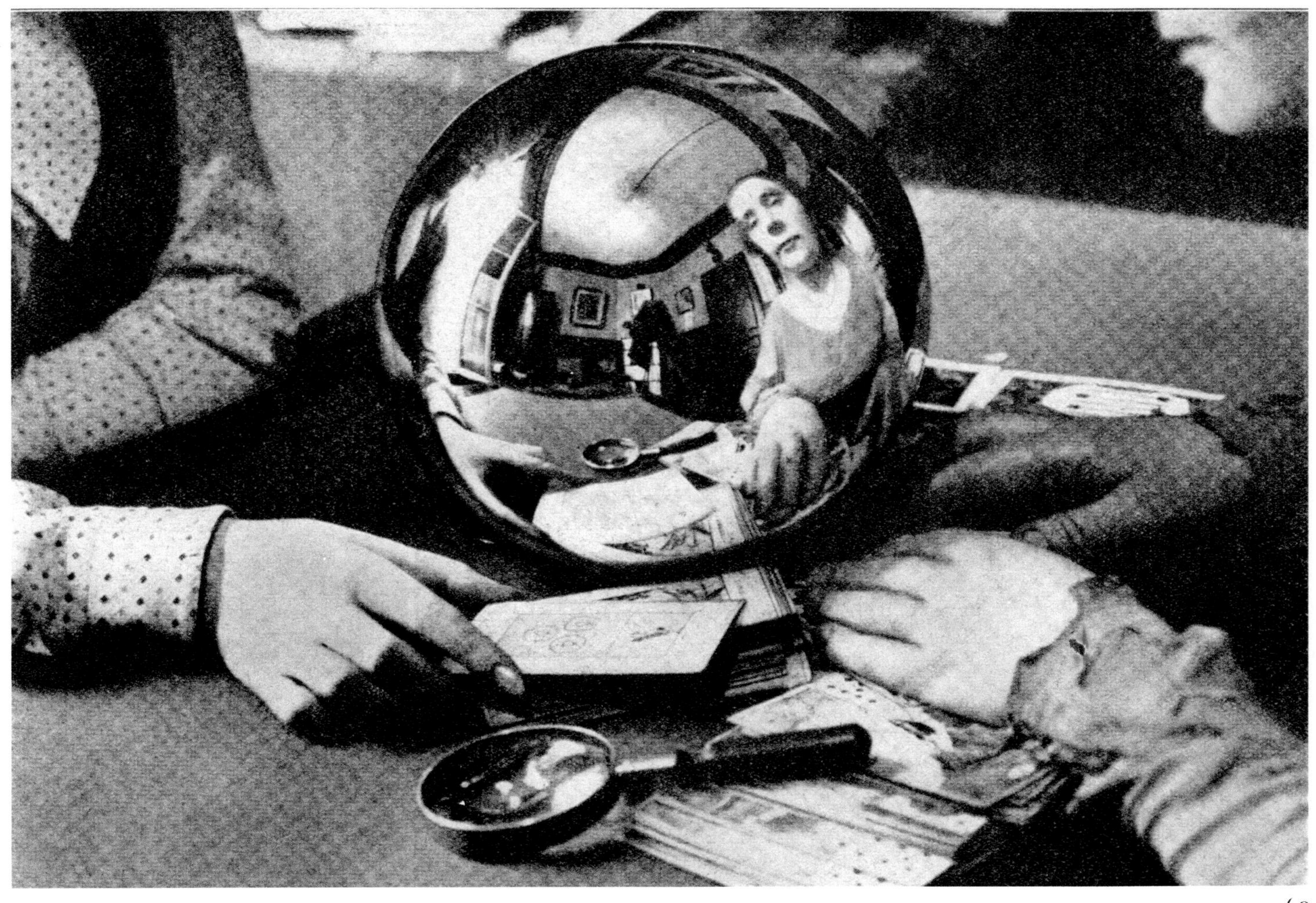

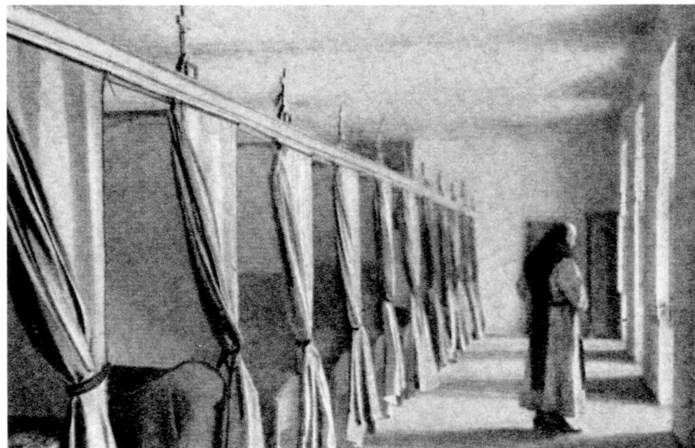

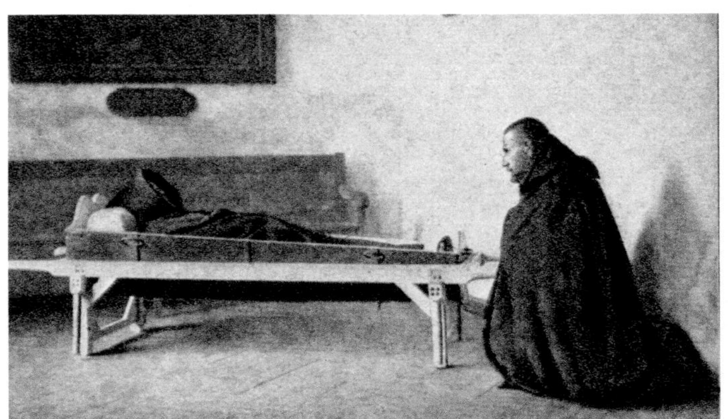

Umbo

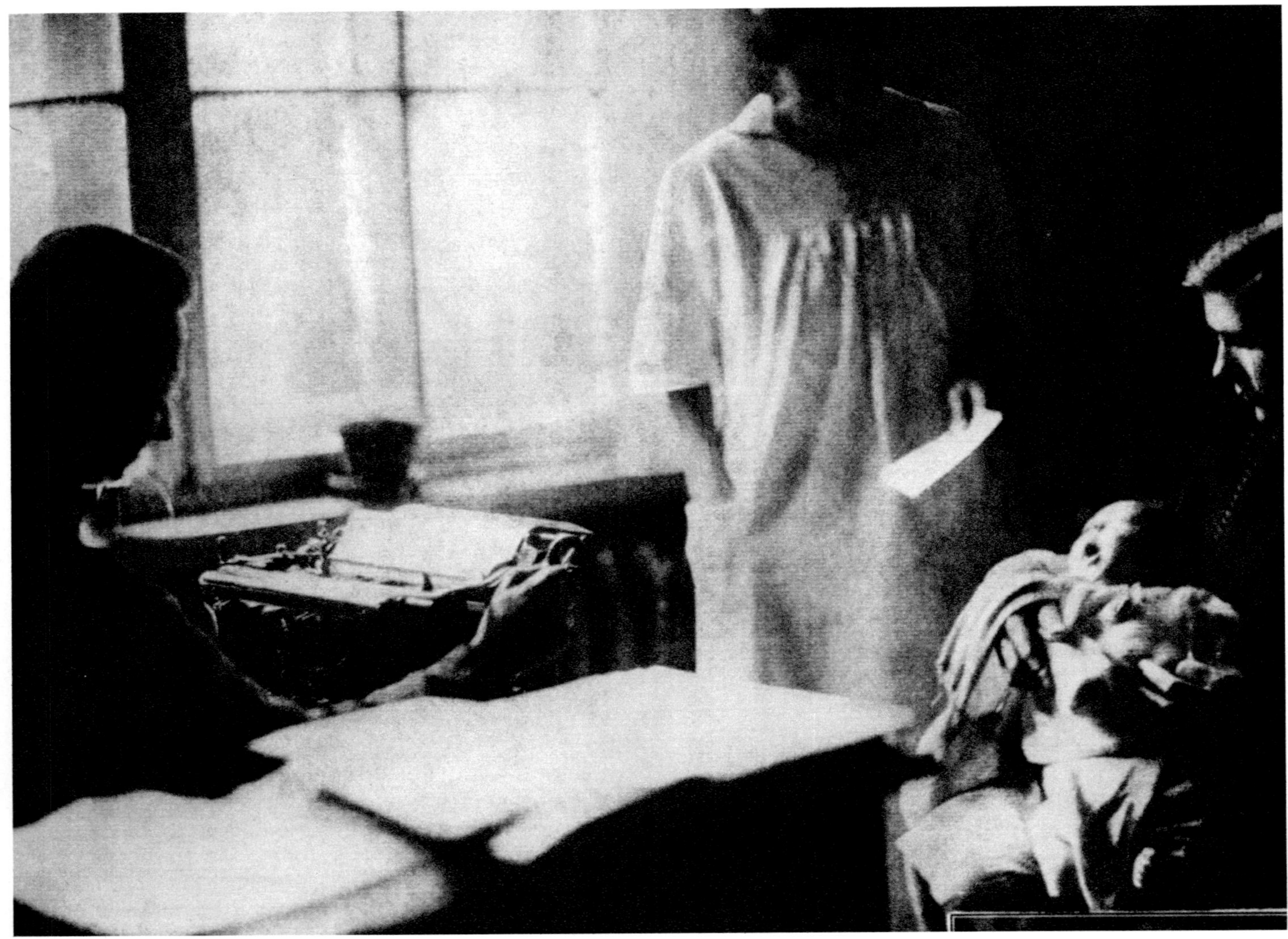

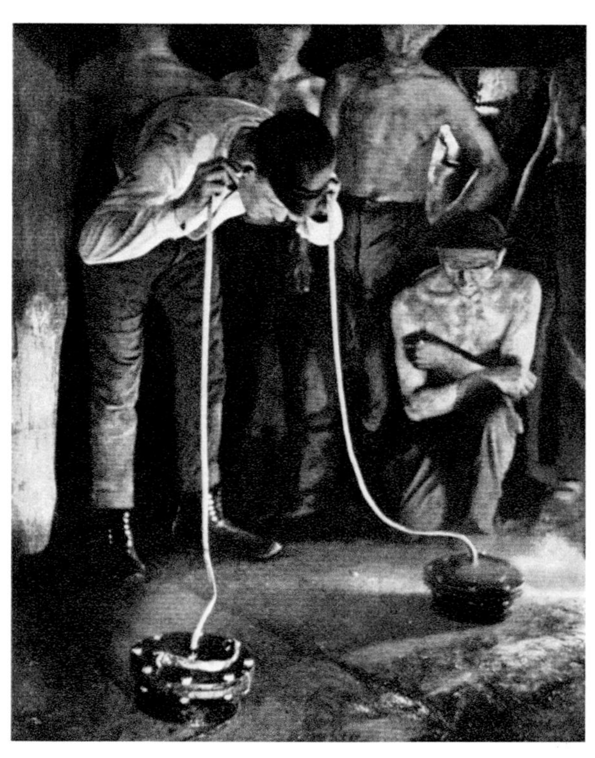

Interessante Aufnahme eines Luftakrobaten beim Hinabklettern in das Fangnetz.

Diese Aufnahmen von der Arbeit der Luftakrobaten wurden wohl zum ersten Male von einem Fotografen gemacht, der seinen Standort dicht über dem in der Kuppel des Varietésaals schwebenden Trapez hatte.

Die Aufnahme zeigt die „Kreuz-Passage“: die Artisten, die Brüder Zemgano, wechseln die Geräte seitlich nebeneinander vorbeifliegend.

Der Artist fliegt, sich 1½mal um die eigene Körperachse drehend, von einem Trapez zum andern.
Fot. Umbo-Dephot.

DER FOTOGRAF 2 METER über dem TRAPEZ

Die Kreuz-Passage von unten gesehen.
Aufnahmen im Berliner Wintergarten.

Harald Lechenperg

E BISHER
ANN
EITEN
EHR
Z. ERSCHEINT AB NR. 27 ZWANZIGSEI
JAHRGANG VIII 1929
NR. 25
20 Pf.
15 Kon.
40 Gr.
30 Cent.
A-I-Z
DIE ARBEITER ZEITUNG ALLER LÄNDER
PUDOWKIN
der berühmte Regisseur von „Sturm über Asien" und der „Letzten Tage von St. Petersburg" prüft die Filmstreifen des neuen deutsch-russischen Gemeinschaftsfilms der Meschrabpom-Prometheus
„Das Leben ist schön"

ERSCHEINT WOCHENTLICH EINMAL • PREIS 20 PFG., Kc. 1,60, 30 GR., 30 SCHWEIZER RP., IN NORDAMERIKA UND KANADA 10 CENTS • V.b.b. • NEUER DEUTSCHER VERLAG, BERLIN W8 • JAHRGANG XII • NR. 9 • 26. 2. 1933

AUS DEM INHALT DIESER NUMMER:

Die Einheitsfront marschiert • Lebensmittel werden teurer • Eine Familie - und Millionen Andere. Wer zerstört die Familie? • 6 Tage - wieder 12 Tote • Sozialismus: Kulturaufbau • Im Schweiße deines Angesichts . . . • Staatlich geprüfte Stempelbrüder • Die Katastrophe von Neunkirchen • U. v. a. m.

AMERIKA
IM PRÄSIDENTSCHAFTS-WAHLKAMPF
Ein Alltagsbild aus New York: Der Arbeits- und Obdachlose, der keine andere Ruhestätte hat als eine Bank mitten im Großstadtverkehr, und neben ihm, vollkommen unberührt von dieser schon selbstverständlich gewordenen Erscheinung, eine Dame, die sich schminkt und pudert.
42,5 Prozent der im Jahre 1926 beschäftigten Arbeiter liegen erwerbslos — im buchstäblichen Sinne des Wortes — auf der Straße. Sie erhalten keinerlei Unterstützung. Wenn auf den öffentlichen Bänken kein Platz mehr ist, kampieren sie irgendwo am Straßenrand, ihr Kopfkissen ist ein Stein, ihre Decke ein Zeitungsblatt mit rosenroten Versprechungen einer neuen Konjunktur, wenn man nur brav für Hoover oder Roosevelt stimmt.
. . . und das Symbol einer neuen Zukunft! Durch Wallstreet, durch die Schlagader des Weltkapitalismus zieht der Zug kampfbereiter Arbeiter und Angestellten, die gegen die imperialistischen Kriegshetzer, gegen die Bankfürsten und Börsenhyänen demonstrieren. Sie wollen nicht länger Opfer ihrer verbrecherischen Politik sein. Zum erstenmal geht durch Amerika eine so starke Welle der Empörung, zum erstenmal sammeln sich Millionen um die rote Fahne, aus zahllosen einzelnen Streiks, Demonstrationen, Hungermärschen und Revolten wächst qualvoll, aber unaufhaltsam die rote Einheitsfront der Ausgebeuteten.

1. MAI-FEIER IN HUNAN

1940 Berliner Illustrirte Zeitung Nr. 50

Brüning. MacDonald. Mussolini.

Lloyd George. Briand. Stalin.

Zamora. Hitler. Gandhi.

Redner, über die man am meisten redet

Udet trudelt

Das Flugzeug steigt. In der Tiefe der Flugplatz und viele hundert Menschen, die auf die Kunstflüge warten

Der Motor setzt aus . . .

. . . und in rasendem Tempo trudelt das Flugzeug ab

Eine der atemraubendsten Vorführungen des bekannten Kunstfliegers Udet ist das „Trudeln". Der Motor des Flugzeuges, das bis zu einer bestimmten Höhe gestiegen ist, wird vom Piloten abgestellt. Durch Verlegung des Schwerpunktes und geschickte Steuerung des Flugzeuges sackt dasselbe mit sich stetig steigender Geschwindigkeit ab. Große Beherrschung des Apparates und äußerste Konzentration sind erforderlich, das Flugreug kurz über dem Erdboden wieder in die normale Flugbahn zurückzureißen

Unser Fotograf ist mit Udet geflogen und hat versucht, seine Erlebnisse beim Trudeln im Bilde festzuhalten. Hier sind seine Bilder. Er selbst aber teilte uns im Vertrauen mit, daß diese Trudelfahrt seine erste und . . . letzte gewesen sei.

Nr. 11 Berliner Illustrirte Zeitung 307

WAHLFIEBER

Berlin im Wahlfieber: Die großen Kundgebungen der Parteien in den Tagen vor der Reichspräsidentenwahl.

Die Kommunisten, die Nationalsozialisten und die „Eiserne Front" im Lustgarten Unter den Linden und eine Kundgebung des „Stahlhelms" im Sportpalast. Die Wahlpropaganda bediente sich diesmal besonders stark der Flugzeuge zum Abwerfen von Wahlaufrufen.

The Photographers

WALTER BOSSHARD (born November 8, 1892 in Samstagern, near Zürich, Switzerland) studied educational theory and the history of art around the end of World War I. His travels took him to Sumatra, Siam, India, and the Far East. In India he met the German photographer and Asia explorer, Emil Trinkler, who asked him to join his expedition to Central Asia. The route led from Srinagar and Kashmir over numerous Himalaya passes through western Tibet to Jarkand and Kashgar in Chinese Turkistan, from 1927 to 1929. After his return via Andizhan and Tashkent in Russian Turkistan, he compiled notes on his travel experiences and evaluated and sorted his photographs.

This expedition, and his subsequent travels to India (1929–30) for the *Münchner Illustrierte Presse*, to China and to Mongolia for the Ullstein publishers, provide us with enduring impressions of encounters with political and military figures such as Chiang Kai-shek and Mao Tse-tung. This expedition made him an undisputed authority on the Far East—in experience and photographs.

As photoreporter for the Ullstein publishing house, Bosshard participated in the Arctic flight of the airship *Graf Zeppelin* in the summer of 1932. After the liquidation of the old Ullstein firm, he worked for American agencies and, from 1939, for the *Neue Zürcher Zeitung* exclusively. Commissioned by this important Swiss newspaper, he traveled extensively through the Balkan countries and the Near East during World War II and subsequently in Africa and the United States. In 1945, he covered the conference for the founding of the United Nations held in San Francisco.

After his return to Switzerland, Bosshard wrote his *Erlebte Weltgeschichte*, and in 1946 he set out once more for Japan and China. Bosshard had lived in Peking until the Communist victory in 1949, when a large part of his photographic material was lost. His activities as a political reporter came to an end in 1953 due to a serious accident in Panmunjon, Korea. Since 1961, Bosshard has been living, to quote his own words, "in the mild climate of southern Spain."

BOOKS: *Durch Tibet und Turkestan* (1942), *Indien kämpft*, *Grünes Grasland Mongolei* (all out of print).

FELIX H. MAN (born November 30, 1893) is described as follows by Bernd Lohse (*Camera*, April 1967): "Hans Baumann, an art student from Freiburg im Breisgau, who had become a journalistic draftsman in Berlin, constantly used the new photographic means, week after week, to produce complete and psychologically sound picture essays in the pages of the great illustrated magazines under the pseudonym of Felix H. Man."

Ever since 1914, when he was drafted into the army, Man recorded his war experiences with a pocket camera. After the war, he resumed his art studies at the Kunstgewerbeschule in Munich, where, in the following decades, he devoted himself wholeheartedly to photojournalism.

From 1929 he worked as production director of photojournalism for Dephot, the German photo service.* In the two years which followed, more than eighty of his reportages appeared in the *Münchner Illustrierte* alone, among them his first "available light" night reportage. He interviewed the great personalities of his time such as Mussolini, Stravinsky, Max Slevogt, Max Liebermann, and George Bernard Shaw, and he created travel reportages on Libya, Tunisia, the United States, Canada, the Arctic, and the Pacific. In 1934, Man moved to London, becoming an important collaborator on the *Weekly Illustrated*, *Lilliput* (1937), and a chief photographer at *Picture Post* from 1938 until the end of the war.

In 1948, Man's first color reportage appeared in *Picture Post*, followed in 1951 by a comprehensive report in *Life* on the Festival of Britain. His interests in contemporary art and in the history of lithography continue unabated. As one of the "fathers of modern picture journalism," he was made an honorary member of the *Deutsche Gesellschaft für Photographie* (German Photographic Society) and received the Cultural Award in 1965 as well as the Federal Services Cross First Class. He now lives in Rome and is cultural correspondent for *Die Welt*.

BOOKS include: *Eight European Artists* (1953); *Über die Anfänge der Lithographie in England* (1967); *Artists' Lithographs* (1970); eight portfolios *Europäische Graphik* since 1963, edited by Man.

EXHIBITIONS: Cologne, Hamburg, Munich, and Freiburg im Breisgau.

ERICH SALOMON (1886–1944) is described by Bernd Lohse as a "Berlin lawyer who, aided by the new Ermanox, was an important explorer in this developing segment of photography. Adept in capturing parliament, law-court scenes, and meetings of important personages, he was always prepared to seize the 'unobserved moment' with ingenuity, boldness, and journalistic flair. He would not use flash powder which had previously been indispensable for interior photographs."

To Erich Salomon, every possible trick was justified in order to photograph the important men of his time, in particular the statesmen who were the prime movers of the great international political events of the twenties and thirties. He would conceal his camera in a hat in which he had made a peephole for the lens, on a telegraph pole or a fire escape ladder, and would arrange to be invited as a guest at banquets at the Royal Academy, discreet, inconspicuous, in tails and white tie.

Salomon's first pictures appeared in Ullstein publications for which he was under contract for a time. Many of his photos were published in *Illustrations* and *Vu* in Paris and in the *Wereldkroniek* and other Dutch publications; also in *Fortune*, *Time*, and *The New York Times*, mainly in 1930 and 1932; and in the *Daily Telegraph* and other London publications between 1935 and 1939. As early as 1931, Salomon was regarded as the first candid camera man of his time, a time which he captured in technically brilliant and carefully composed documents.

He and members of his family died in Auschwitz concentration camp in 1944.

BOOKS: *Berühmte Zeitgenossen in unbewachten Augenblicken* (1931); *Portrait of an Age* (New York, 1963).

EXHIBITIONS: Between 1953 and 1963 in London, Cologne, Berlin, Hamburg, Leiden, Stuttgart, Rochester, New York City, and Washington, D.C.

BIBLIOGRAPHY: Beaumont Newhall, *The History of Photography* (New York, 1938); Helmut Gernsheim, *The History of Photography* (London, 1955); Peter Pollack, *The Picture History of Photography* (New York, 1958); Wilson Hicks, *Words and Pictures* (New York, 1952).

WOLFGANG WEBER (born June 17, 1902 in Leipzig) studied ethnography and musicology. The Phonetic Institute of Berlin University commissioned him to travel to Kilimanjaro to study and record the music

---

* Felix Man comments as follows on the history of Dephot: «The German photo service was founded in 1928 by Simon Gutmann and Alfred Marx. Originally an agency for pictures and news with a running dispatch service, one year later, under the direction of Felix H. Man (production director of the picture reportage section) and Umbo (director of the studio for portraits and advertising photography), and in close collaboration with Stefan Lorant (one-time Berlin editor of the *Münchner Illustrierte Presse*) it became the center of modern photojournalism.

Kurt Hübschmann (Hutton) joined Dephot in 1929. At first a studio and advertising photographer, he subsequently became a photojournalist. This same "school" of the first photojournalists was also "attended" by Lechenperg and Cohnitz.
After having been converted into a limited company with Simon Gutmann, Umbo, Dr. von Roque, and Felix H. Man as partners—virtually a forerunner of Magnum—Dephot discontinued its activities as a news agency in 1932–3.»

of the Chagga tribe. His first written articles and photos on the situation of the Negroes were at first cultural in interest, later political. The accent in his style of presentation changed gradually from the written word to the phototext report. Photojournalistic work by Weber which appeared at this time includes "Struggle with the Desert" (Africa) and "Foreign Industry on the Battlefields" (France), both of which were published in the *Berliner Illustrirte*. He also did a lot of work for Ullstein. He held the post of reporter-in-chief for "Wort und Bild" on the *Münchner Illustrierte Presse* but after a few years returned to the *Berliner Illustrirte*. During the war, he created reportages on neutral soil for all the belligerents and was the only reporter to accompany Italo Balbo's squadron flight over the Atlantic. He was reporter-in-chief on the first postwar illustrated magazine, the *Neue Illustrierte*. Armed with camera and ballpoint pen, Weber is present wherever there is a crisis. Since 1955, the countries of the Third World have been his special field, and from this date on he has worked in collaboration with Madeleine Beck. The themes and places of his reporting activities are the Congo and the Suez crises, North and South America, the South Seas, the North Pole, meetings with Nehru and Chou En-lai. His most important photoreportage is "New York–Moscow." The change in the structure of magazines in Germany since 1964 led Weber to go over to television for which he contributes travel reports. He has also presented the theme of the white man in South Africa and Rhodesia in an instructive text and photoreport in the *Bunte* and the *Schweizer Illustrierte*.

Wolfgang Weber is an honorary member of the German Photographic Society. Weber's biography closes characteristically with the laconic remark: "May 15, 1972: Guest of Fidel Castro and Boumedienne in Algiers."

Books: *Hotel Affenbrotbaum*; *Abenteuer einer Kamera*; *Barcelona—Weltstadt im Werden*; *Abenteuer meines Lebens*; *Auf Abwegen um die Welt*.

MARTIN MUNKACSI (born May 18, 1896 near Kolozsvar, Hungary, died on July 14, 1963 in New York) started as a painter. At the age of seventeen he went to Budapest where, in a year, he became a sports reporter for the *AZ EST*. The subsequent course of his life was largely the result of a stroke of fate: in 1932 he took a picture of men in a heated discussion, and this picture decided the fate of a falsely accused man—as well as Munkacsi's own. He became a photoreporter and one year later was the best-paid man in the field.

In 1927 Munkacsi presented himself unannounced at the Ullstein offices in Berlin. There he remained for three years in the capacity of photojournalist. His work was published in *BIZ*, *Dame*, *Studio* (London), and in commercial art. His travels took him to all continents, and he flew "around the world" in the airship *Graf Zeppelin* for the *Berliner Illustrirte*.

Led by the political situation in Germany to renew his previous contact with the Hearst Press, Munkacsi emigrated to the United States. His contract with Hearst was exclusive; Munkacsi's pictures appeared in *Harper's Bazaar*, *Town and Country*, *Good Housekeeping*, and *Pictorial Review*.

He photographed prominent personalities in the fields of art, politics, and society—work which always included the personal element. He constantly improved his photographic technique, developing and processing the films and photos himself throughout his lifetime.

His collaboration with *Life* began with the first issue in 1936, which contained a number of his picture sequences. For the *Ladies Home Journal* he created a series entitled "How America Lives," and his photos appeared regularly in the *US Camera Annuals*. In 1941, he was generally regarded as the best-paid photographer in the United States and the world's best photographer of women.

Munkacsi was probably one of the most versatile talents among photojournalists. He was a writer, motorcycle racer, played football for Hungary, collected antiques, and constructed his own cameras.

Books: *Fool's Apprentice* (1945); *Nudes* (1951).

WILLI RUGE (Unfortunately, despite extensive research, we have been unable to acquire the biographical details of the late Willi Ruge.)

His photoreportages, which appeared in the thirties mainly in the *Berliner Illustrirte Zeitung*, reveal him as a technically outstanding photographer and a daring reporter. His pictures document airplane experiments and records, and his pictures of himself, taken during a parachute jump with the camera tied to him, are particularly famous.

Different, and essentially human, are his pictures of the war in Chaco. As a war reporter—to a certain extent as predecessor of Capa, Bischof, Duncan, *et al.*,—he described the suffering and distress of the fighting forces.

ALFRED EISENSTAEDT (born December 6, 1898 in Dierschau, West Prussia) started experimenting with a folding camera at the age of fourteen. Three years later, he was called to the army, and in 1918, he was wounded. After the war he worked as a salesman, concerning himself with photography only during his spare time. He sold his first picture, in 1927, to the *Weltspiegel*. Two years later, in 1931, he signed a contract as a reporter news photographer with Pacific and Atlantic Photos, an agency which was taken over by Associated Press. Eisenstaedt's first large-scale reportage dealt with the award of the Nobel Prize to Thomas Mann in Stockholm in 1935. After six years of successful experiences as a photoreporter for important European and American magazines and newspapers, Eisenstaedt left Europe for the United States in 1936. A year after *Life* started publication, he became one of four photographers who formed the core of the magazine's original photography department. He created almost 1,300 reportages for *Life*, his pictures appearing on eighty covers. Millions of readers are acquainted with his photographs of royalty, statesmen, writers, scientists, musicians, and stars of stage and film, as well as his pictures of the American Depression and of the home front during World War II. Eisenstaedt was as tireless in his physical activity as in his acquisition of material. Of the Abyssinian invasion alone he made no less than 3,500 negatives (taken with a Leica with 35, 50, and 90 mm lenses). Eisenstaedt is a member of the German Photographic Society, whose Cultural Award he received in 1962.

Awards: 1951, Photographer of the Year by the *Britannica Book of the Year* and the University of Missouri School of Journalism; 1953, The Clifton C. Edom Award for Photographic Achievement; 1961, presented with the 1,000,001 camera by the Leitz firm; 1967, International Understanding Award for Photographic Achievement in Photography; 1968, Distinction in Photography—as One of the World's Ten Great Photographers (by an international opinion poll by *Popular Photography*); 1971, National Press Photographers' Association Joseph A. Sprague Memorial Award.

Books: *Witness to Our Time* (1966); *The Eye of Eisenstaedt*; *Martha's Vineyard*; *Witness to Nature*; *Wimbledon: A Celebration.*

TIM N. GIDAL (born in Munich 1909) studied history, art history, and national economics. In 1929, his first reportage, "Servus Kumpel," appeared in the *Münchner Illustrierte Presse*. He works with Ermanoxes and Leicas, and since 1930, with a 4×4 cm Rollei. His numerous photoreportages have appeared in the *Münchner*, the *Berliner*, the *Kölnische*, the *Neue Illustrierte Zeitung*, *AIZ*, the *Frankfurter Illustrierte*, the *Woche*, and the *Feuerreiter*. His work has taken him to Austria, Italy, Czechoslovakia, and Palestine, where he remained from 1936 to 1938. His first color reportage "Marie-Claire" (Paris) appeared in 1938. From 1938 to 1940, together with Felix H. Man and Hutton (Hübschmann), he was a leading photoreporter on *Picture Post* under the editorship of Stefan Lorant. From 1942 to 1945 he served in the British Army as one of the chief reporters. Sixty-two of his pictures appeared in *Parade*, the official army magazine. Until 1955, he lectured at the New School for Social Research in New York on photoreportage in world history. Tim N. Gidal is one of the leading initiators in the field of German photojournalism. He is an honorary member of the German Photographic Society, a fellow of the Royal Photographic Society, and is currently senior lecturer at the Hebrew University in Jerusalem.

Books: Twenty-three volumes on twenty-three countries created between 1955 and 1970 in collaboration with Sonia Gidal (human interest photoreportages for educational purposes). *Everybody Lives in Communities*, a "humanized geography book for elementary schools."

GEORG GIDAL (born March 13, 1908 in Munich) studied biology and medicine. Together with his brother, Tim N. Gidal, he worked as a photoreporter for many newspapers and magazines. He died in an accident in 1931.

ANDRÉ KERTESZ (born July 2, 1894 in Budapest) attended technical college until 1912. From 1914 to 1918 he served in the Austro-Hungarian army, and in 1915, he was wounded. His first camera was an Ica 4.5 × 6 cm Box, and he photographed his war scenes with a Goerz-Tenax 4.5 × 6 cm camera. In 1916, he was awarded a prize for a satirical self-portrait, and in 1917, his first photos appeared in the magazine *Erdekes Ujsag*. From 1925 to 1928 he lived in Paris and worked for the *Frankfurter Illustrierte*, *Uhu*, the *Berliner Illustrirte Zeitung*, the *Strassburger Illustrierte*, and the *London Times*. After the first exhibition of his work in the gallery Sacre-du-Printemps in Paris, he bought his first Leica, and he was subsequently a guest of the First Independent Salon of Photography. His activities on *Vu* (under Lucien Vogel) began in 1928, and one year later, the Staatliche Museum, the Kunstbibliothek in Berlin, and the King Albert Museum in Zwickau showed interest in his work. Kertesz worked for six years for *Art et Médecine*, and until 1937, he was closely associated with the Keystone Studios. He subsequently worked for *Harper's Bazaar*, *Vogue*, *Town and Country*, *The American Magazine*, *Collier's*, *Coronet*, and *Look*. (Between 1959 and 1962 he was under exclusive contract to Condé Nast Publications.) He has helped to organize countless exhibitions in America and Europe and has received numerous awards.

BOOKS: *Enfants*, text by Jaboune (1933); *Paris vu par André Kertesz*, text by Pierre MacOrlan (1934); *Nos Amis les Bêtes*, text by Jaboune (1936); *Les Cathédrales du Vin*, text by Pierre Hamp (1937); *Day of Paris*, text by George Davis (1945).

BIBLIOGRAPHY: J. Szarkowski, *André Kertesz, Photographer* (1945); Alice Gambier, *André Kertesz: Photographies* (1965); Anna Farova, *André Kertesz* (1966); Robert E. Hood, *12 at War* (including a chapter: "André Kertesz, Soldier and Candid Cameraman in World War I" (1967); *The Concerned Photographer*, edited by Cornell Capa (1968); *On Reading* (1971).

UMBO (OTTO UMBEHR): This photoreporter's short and modest statement about himself reads as follows:

"Born January 18, 1902; from 1921 to 1923 in the Bauhaus, Weimar; first photos, 1926; cofounder of Dephot; photojournalist until 1943, soldier until 1945. Returned impecunious from the war, made a new beginning in Hanover; 1950 some reportages published in *Picture Post*; lecturer at the Werkkunstschule in Hanover since 1965. Honorary member of the German Photographic Society and member of the Deutsche Werkbund."

HARALD LECHENPERG (born 1904) was one of the photojournalists who originated the "candid camera" style of reportage. His first work of importance appeared in 1929 in the *Woche*, the *Leipziger Illustrirte*, the *Miroir du Monde* (Paris), and the *Illustrated London News*. In 1930, he was engaged as a reporter for the Scherl publishers in India, and he provided the international press with the first pictures of the coronation of Nadir Shah in Afghanistan. He made another trip to India for the *Berliner Illustrirte*, and he subsequently lived and worked as a text-and-photo journalist in Africa, Arabia, and North America. From 1937 to 1949 he was editor-in-chief on *BIZ*, the style and presentation of which he considerably modernized. After the war he became editor-in-chief of *Quick* and *Weltbild*. Lechenperg regards the production of documentary films for television as an extension and intensification of photojournalism, and he now devotes himself exclusively to this field. His favorite subject is Asia.

ROMEO E. MARTINEZ. As editor of this series, Romeo E. Martinez crowns an almost forty-year career as journalist and picture director.

Martinez was chief of the illustration departments with the magazines *Vu* and *Excelsior* in Paris and is a member of the *Conseil en illustrations de la "Grande Encyclopédie française."* His ten years as editor-in-chief of the monthly magazine *Camera* in Lucerne contributed greatly to the international success of this journal. He has been responsible for the organization of the biennial of photography in Venice.

The selection of these pictures was made from the German illustrated press of the twenties and thirties (above all from the *Berliner Illustrirte Zeitung* and the *Münchner Illustrierte Presse*). Their authenticity is guaranteed—without exception, they have been previously published.

The reproduction of whole pages in facsimile, complete with the original captions, serves to show the events of the time as well as the style of presentation.

The exact wording of the captions was, with few exceptions, taken from the original publication.

Captions to the pictures

WALTER BOSSHARD

Page 31: Pictures of the expedition to Central Asia 1927–9. The Zeldar of Saktis (top). The march into the unknown (bottom left). Yaks as beasts of burden; Sanju-Dawan Pass, October 18, 1929 (bottom right).

Page 32: The man who challenged the British Empire. Mahatma Gandhi reading.

Page 33: The last photos before Gandhi's arrest. Gandhi reading a satirical English poem about himself (top). Gandhi taking a midday nap (bottom left). Gandhi eating onion soup (bottom right). Published 1929–30.

Page 34: Polar flight with the Zeppelin after Umberto Nobile's unsuccessful expedition. View from the airship of the ice-breaker *Malygin* in Hooker Bay (top). On the way from the *Malygin* to the Zeppelin (center). How the Russian visitors from the *Malygin* saw the Zeppelin (bottom).

Page 35: Dr. Eckener in the cabin of the airship. Land which no human foot had trod: a newly discovered island, previously Nicholas II Land (bottom left). Published 1931.

Page 36: Kumbum, the city of three thousand monks in China. The professor of medical science and morals (top left). Medical exams in individual cells (top right). Evening meditation (bottom). Published 1934.

FELIX H. MAN

Page 37: Evening discussion in The Hague (Foreign Minister Stresemann, the speaker for the German delegation at The Hague Conference, with the German ambassador Count Zech). Published 1929.

Pages 38–9: Between midnight and dawn on the Kurfürstendamm. An excursion with the camera through the west main street of Berlin. Published 1929.

Pages 40–1: "Filmstar for 1.50 mark" (photos taken in a Berlin dramatic school). Published 1930.

ERICH SALOMON

Page 42: September 1931, the first time after World War I that French statesmen visited Germany: Ministers Briand and Laval. The top photo was taken from the outside through the window. Recognizable here are Dr. Brüning, Briand, Fernand Léger, and Philippe Berthelot.

Pages 42–3: Summit conference in 1928 (bottom). Aristide Briand and Gustav Stresemann met the British foreign minister Sir August Chamberlain in Lugano. From left to right: Zaleski, Poland; Adatei, Japan; Chamberlain; Stresemann; Briand; Scialoja, Italy.

Page 43: In July 1931, the German and French delegations traveled, by train especially provided by the French government, from Paris to London for the Seven Power Conference. (Top) From left to right: Philippe Berthelot, Chancellor Brüning, the Belgian foreign minister Paul Hymans, the German foreign minister Dr. Curtius, Briand, Laval, and André-François Poncet.

Page 44: League of Nations meeting in 1928: the Rumanian poetess and League of Nations delegate Varescu during a lively speech appealing for peace (top). (Bottom) Two women politicians in 1930: Katharina von Kardorf-Oheimb, wife of German delegate, and Ada Schmidt-Beil.

Page 45: The High Court in London, 1929. At left above is Justice Avory, at right the Lord Chief Justice Lord Hewart. After the death of his friend Avory, Lord Hewart gave permission for the publication of this picture, although the taking of pictures in court and the publication of photos of this kind are punishable offenses in England.

Page 46: Wilhelm Furtwängler conducting in The Hague, 1932. After another concert in Brussels not only Furtwängler, but also Salomon, was introduced to the Queen Mother Elizabeth. "Oh," she said to the photographer, "I was wondering all through the concert what instrument you were going to play."

Page 47: Marlene Dietrich telephoning her daughter from Hollywood. (This sequence probably appeared for the first time in 1930 in Ullstein's *Blatt der Hausfrau.* Reproduced from Salomon's *Portrait of an Age.*)

WOLFGANG WEBER

Pages 48–9: From the series "Village Without Work." This is how the Franconian families were obliged to live: Under a roof with loose and broken tiles (left). "... and now our men are out of work... we shall have to pull through by taking in work (right). The whole family works for a week on a piece of material like this... On Saturday we will be paid four or five marks for it...."

Page 49: "We don't want crisis money or relief... only work, any work—on the land, on the street, anything." Published 1931.

Pages 50–1: The race for diamonds, scenes experienced by Wolfgang Weber at the opening of a new diamond field in South Africa. Feverish tension (top). The starter's shot, for which four thousand men and women are waiting (bottom).

Page 51: The frantic race over thousands of yards to the most advantageous spot (top). At the finish (bottom). Published 1934.

Page 52: Impressions of travels in Scotland. Highland dancing, clans, kilts, and tartans. Published 1930.

MARTIN MUNKACSI

Page 53: The newspaper king Hearst entertaining (left). The Prince of Wales in his reception room in St. James' Palace, London (top right). Wedding celebration in the house of Mustafa Kemal Pasha in Ankara (bottom right). The President of the Turkish Republic opening the dance with the bride, his adopted daughter Nibile Hanum. Published 1929, 1933, 1934.

Page 54: Four weeks in the modern Negroe state of Liberia. The old and the new Liberia: A mother fetching her son from school (top). On the way to church in the capital city of Monrovia (bottom).

Page 55: Liberian youths. Published 1931.

Page 56: Coffee tragedy—a million pounds of coffee thrown into the sea (Munkacsi's first report from his South American trip). A desperate deed: the mountain of coffee is mixed with tar and pressed into fuel material (top left). Brazil is smothered with coffee (top right). The coffee being shoveled into the sea. Published 1932.

Page 57: From a special issue of *BIZ* of March 21, 1933, devoted to celebrations at the opening of the German parliament. March of the German army (left). The best spectators' positions were reserved for the veteran soldiers of 1870–1 (right). The "eye of the world," the movie camera, can be seen behind the veterans.

WILLI RUGE

Page 58: War in Chaco. The "invisible" jungle soldiers (top). On patrol in the "green hell" (bottom).

Page 59: Inconveniences of jungle warfare: Scratched by thorns (top left). Comradeship in the wilderness: a soldier carrying his wounded comrade for miles to the field hospital (top right). He died of thirst (bottom). Published 1934.

Page 60: From the special issue of *BIZ*, May 1, 1933: in the Zeppelin above the festivities. View from the airship of one of the motor balloons. From here a radio report was broadcast to the whole of Germany on the fantastic march of the masses.

Page 61: Lola Schröter, who established a new world record in parachute jumping, making a parachute jump from a height of 18,000 feet. A few minutes before the jump—a gulp of oxygen (top). Ruge went up with her in the airplane (bottom). Published 1932.

ALFRED EISENSTAEDT

Page 62: The London slums, taken in Whitechapel. Englishwomen unrecognizable as such (top). They gather here from all over the world (bottom left). A man and wife from Whitechapel (bottom right).

Page 63: Joyless street (top). The next generation (center). They spend their youth here (bottom). Published 1932.

Page 64: "Semper eleganti"—relief of a policeman by his colleague in front of the Palazzo Chigi in Rome (top left). Underground manicure salon in Milan (top right). In the Mussolini Forum, at that time the newest and finest stadium in the world (bottom left). In the Palazzo Massimo (bottom right). Published 1933; and 1966 in *Witness to Our Time.*

Page 65: On the way to the "Monastery in the Clouds." An excursion to the famous mountain monastery in Thessaly. A monastery of great seclusion (left). One of the five monks looking out of a window (top right). The other, no less dangerous approach to the monastery; the ladder, in contrast to the rope, by which Eisenstaedt was pulled up (bottom right). Published 1934.

TIM N. GIDAL

Page 66: Hamburg by night. Chinese sailors (top). A shot has been fired (bottom left). Prostitutes' street (bottom right). Published 1930.

Page 67: Servus Kumpel! The brotherhood of vagabonds meets in Stuttgart. Published 1929.

Page 68: Israel: new colony near Rehoboth (top). Jerusalem, the Wailing Wall (bottom left). Palestine: English troops guarding the railway line (bottom right). Published 1930.

ANDRÉ KERTESZ

Page 69: Portrait of a famous fortune teller in her consulting room (fortune tellers like to be mysteriously veiled) (top). Part of her equipment is the "magic crystal ball of Cagliostro" in which, according to ancient superstition, the future is reflected (bottom). Published 1930.

Pages 70–1: The House of Silence. The Motherhouse of the Trappist order, Notre-Dame de la Grande Trappe, in Soligny. Monks on the way to mass (left).

Page 71: Lay brothers at mass (right, top to bottom). Mealtime—the monks are vegetarians. The monks' dormitory; the first cell is inhabited by the abbot; each cubicle is marked with the initials of the monk. When one of the brothers dies, a three-day vigil is kept by the open coffin. Published 1929.

UMBO

Page 72: Children for adoption. A visit to an adoption center in Berlin. In the dormitory (top). The moment of parting (bottom). Published 1929.

Page 73: Mine disaster. Listening for signs of life (top). The search for the buried miners in the central mine near Beuthen. The rescue team works with "geophones." This picture was taken at a depth of 2,000 feet. The rescuers (bottom). This picture was taken on the tenth day after the catastrophe during the evening shift. The miners worked in eight-hour shifts. Published 1932.

Page 74: The Zemgano brothers demonstrate their skill. The photographer is positioned six feet above the trapeze. These pictures of acrobats were probably the first ever to have been taken from above the swaying trapeze.

HARALD LECHENPERG

Page 75: Christians in the jungle. An Indian land worker in one of Goa's old churches (left). Cross and saint sculpture in a village in Goa (top right). Indian acolyte (bottom right). Published 1933.

Page 76: Car trip *par excellence*: Bombay–Berlin. In front of a Buddhist statue by the roadside in Gwalio (top left). In the desert sand of Belutschistan (top right). In the slime of the Tapti River between Bombay and Delhi (bottom).

Page 77: Ferry across the river (top). Encounter on the Indian highway (bottom). Published 1933.

AIZ

Page 78: Pudovkin, the famous director of *Storm over Asia* and *The Last Days of St. Petersburg*, examining the film strips of the new joint German-Russian film *Das Leben ist schön*. (VIII, 1929)

Page 79: "For work, bread, and freedom. All working women vote for List 3!" An example of aggressive election propaganda by the *Arbeiter Illustrierte Zeitung* (XII, 1931).

Page 80: The Capitalist. Photomontage by John Heartfield (XI, 1932).

Page 81: United States during the presidential elections.

Page 82: Photo of the headquarters of the Cantonese army. Spring 1926, Chiang Kai-shek, his wife, Borodin, and Ku-Ming Fu are among those pictured (top). May Day festivities in Hunan (bottom).

MISCELLANEOUS

Page 83: The speakers who are most spoken about: Brüning, MacDonald, Mussolini, Lloyd George, Briand, Stalin, Zamora, Hitler, and Gandhi. Published 1931, reprinted from *Vanity Fair*.

Page 84: Student unrest abroad. Politics in universities. Warsaw, police suppression of street demonstration by students, with water from hydrants (top left). Athens, students demonstrating, armed with battens and truncheons, in favor of the annexation of Cyprus to Greece (top right). Prague, Czechoslovakian students being dispersed by the police after a demonstration against the admittance of foreigners as medical students (bottom). Published 1932.

Page 85: Examples of photographic blur as a means of expressive impact. Published 1930.

Page 86: Election fever in Berlin. The party demonstrations shortly before the election of the president. Published 1932.

Page 87: Reichstag fire, February 1933.

Page 88: Georgi M. Dimitrov, the Bulgarian Communist leader, falsely accused and unsuccessfully tried by the Nazis for the Reichstag fire (top). Göring testifying at the trial (bottom).

Page 89: Van der Lubbe and Torgler, also on trial for the Reichstag fire (top). The courtroom during the trial (bottom).

Page 90: Hitler's political opponents were interned in so-called protective custody camps. Oranienburg in the spring of 1933 (top). Published in 1964 in *Das Dritte Reich in Bildern und Dokumenten*, Volume I. Adolf Hitler walking through rows of hundreds of thousands of supporters to the podium on Bückeberg near Hameln—a kind of "harvest thanksgiving" celebration (bottom). Published 1934.

Index

f. = following page;
ff. = following pages